# The Fine Art of Interviewing

# The Fine Art of Interviewing

**JAMES G. GOODALE**

*Partner*
*Philbrook, Goodale Associates*
*Houston, Texas*

Prentice-Hall, Inc., Englewood Cliffs, N.J. 07632

*Library of Congress Cataloging in Publication Data*

GOODALE, JAMES G.
    The fine art of interviewing.

    Includes bibliographical references and index.
    1. Employment interviewing.  I. Title.
HF5549.I6G6        658.3'1124        81–10716
ISBN  0-13-317008-X        AACR2

Editorial/production supervision and interior design by Kim Gueterman
Manufacturing buyer: Ed O'Dougherty

Printed in the United States of America

10  9  8  7  6  5  4  3  2

ISBN 0-13-317008-X

PRENTICE-HALL INTERNATIONAL, INC., *London*
PRENTICE-HALL OF AUSTRALIA PTY. LIMITED, *Sydney*
PRENTICE-HALL OF CANADA, LTD., *Toronto*
PRENTICE-HALL OF INDIA PRIVATE LIMITED, *New Delhi*
PRENTICE-HALL OF JAPAN, INC., *Tokyo*
PRENTICE-HALL OF SOUTHEAST ASIA PTE. LTD., *Singapore*
WHITEHALL BOOKS LIMITED, *Wellington, New Zealand*

*To Robin*

# Contents

**PREFACE**   *xiii*

# 1

### INTRODUCTION   *1*

THE IMPORTANCE OF INTERVIEWS   2

GAME PLAYING IN THE INTERVIEW   4

CONSEQUENCES OF POOR INTERVIEWING   5

THE ART OF INTERVIEWING   7

    Content   8

    Conducting   10

INTERVIEWING SKILLS AND TECHNIQUES   13

    Nondirective Techniques   13

    Directive Techniques   16

    The Interviewer   17

THE PERSONAL TOUCH   18

THE PLAN OF THIS BOOK   19

# 2

## SELECTION INTERVIEWING   *21*

OBJECTIVES   22

CORRECTING THE SELECTION INTERVIEW'S
  WEAKNESSES   24

    Poor versus Proper Planning   26

    The Interviewer as Amateur Psychiatrist   28

    Subjectivity in Evaluating Applicants' Potential
      to Perform   32

    Interviewers' Bias   32

    Building a Better Interview   33

DESIGNING A TAILORED INTERVIEW   34

SELECTION INTERVIEWING AND THE LAW   40

IMPLICATIONS OF EEO LEGISLATION   41

EFFECTS OF EEO LEGISLATION ON SELECTION
  INTERVIEWING   43

    Information Collected in the Interview   43

    What Can Be Asked?   46

    Basis for the Evaluation   47

    Data Retention   48

CONDUCTING THE SELECTION INTERVIEW   49

    Preparation for the Interview   49

    During the Interview   52

    Additional Reminders   56

GUIDE FOR GATHERING INFORMATION   58

THE BOTTOM LINE   62

# 3

## PERFORMANCE APPRAISAL INTERVIEWING   *65*

OBJECTIVES   66

IMPROVING THE PERFORMANCE APPRAISAL
  INTERVIEW   68

APPRAISING PERFORMANCE OR RESULTS   75

MAKING FEEDBACK USEFUL   78

PLANNING SUCCESSFUL PERFORMANCE APPRAISAL
  INTERVIEWS   82

CONDUCTING THE PERFORMANCE APPRAISAL
  INTERVIEW   82

    Approach   82

    The Risks   86

    An Alternative: Problem Solve and Tell   89

    Before the Interview   89

    During the Interview   90

INTERVIEW STYLE, SUPERVISORY STYLE, AND
  ORGANIZATION CLIMATE   95

INTERVIEW TRANSCRIPT   96

# 4

## COUNSELING INTERVIEWING   *105*

HELP IS A SCARCE COMMODITY   107

OBJECTIVES   108

INTERACTION OF COUNSELOR AND CLIENT   109

    Approach   111

    Format   113

    A Note of Caution   114

CONDUCTING THE COUNSELING INTERVIEW  115

MANAGING THE COUNSELING INTERVIEW  121

# 5

## CAREER PLANNING INTERVIEWING  *123*

DEFINITION OF CAREER PLANNING  125

THE MANAGER'S ROLE IN CAREER PLANNING  126

OBJECTIVES  127

PLANNING THE CAREER PLANNING INTERVIEW  141

    Approach  141

    Before the Interview  141

    Format  143

CONDUCTING THE CAREER PLANNING INTERVIEW  144

CAREER PLANNING AND PERFORMANCE APPRAISAL  147

OUTPLACEMENT  148

THE PROTEAN CAREER  148

# 6

## DISCIPLINARY INTERVIEWING  *151*

WHY DISCIPLINARY INTERVIEWS ARE NECESSARY  152

OBJECTIVES  153

PLANNING THE DISCIPLINARY INTERVIEW  155

    Approach  155

    Before the Interview  155

    Format  157

CONDUCTING THE DISCIPLINARY INTERVIEW   158

   Don'ts of Disciplinary Interviewing   163

   Do's of Disciplinary Interviewing   164

REDUCING THE NEED FOR DISCIPLINARY
INTERVIEWS   166

# 7

## EXIT INTERVIEWING   *169*

SUCCESS AND FAILURE OF EXIT INTERVIEWS   170

OBJECTIVES   171

PLANNING THE EXIT INTERVIEW   172

   Approach   172

   Before the Interview   173

   Format   176

CONDUCTING THE EXIT INTERVIEW   177

   Don'ts of Exit Interviewing   179

   Do's of Exit Interviewing   180

AFTER THE INTERVIEW   182

AN OUNCE OF PREVENTION   185

INTERVIEW TRANSCRIPT   185

**INDEX**   *197*

# *Preface*

This is a book about how to interview. It is written primarily for working people who conduct interviews with job applicants and their own employees. If you are a supervisor, manager, or personnel specialist, or an employee or student aspiring to these positions, you will find the book useful. The book includes six kinds of interviews commonly conducted in the business world: selection, performance appraisal, counseling, career planning, disciplinary, and exit.

I have tried to keep the writing clear, practical, and free of academic jargon. Although the book draws on a broad body of research in applied psychology and business management, the material it contains can be readily applied. I have included basic principles on how to plan and conduct each interview along with examples and illustrations. My intention is to give you the fundamentals which, with practice, will enable you to conduct skillful, effective interviews.

The key to any approach to skill training is flexibility. When treating each type of interview, I have not presented long lists of questions to be asked. There is no magic set of questions which constitutes an ideal interview. Rather, I have presented an approach to planning and conducting interviews, with specific guidelines and steps for you to follow. My goal is to provide guidance but still allow you the flexibility to adjust to the situation, the interviewee, and your own personal style.

In addition to technical material, I have included two topics of concern to anyone who has to conduct interviews in today's business world. The first is game playing done by well-trained and well-rehearsed interviewees. Especially in selection interviews, we have entered the age of the professional interviewee who baffles inexperienced interviewers and often prevents them from obtaining needed information. The book emphasizes how you can cut through the game playing and get to the real person you are interviewing.

A second topic of concern is the impact which civil rights legislation and the Equal Employment Opportunity Commission have had on interviewing. Personality and personal bias can strongly influence interviewers' perceptions and judgments of interviewees. Especially in selection and performance appraisal interviews, unskillful interviewers may find themselves and their employers open to charges of discrimination. I have reviewed the relevance of recent legislation on interviewing and have included approaches and techniques to minimize your liability under this legislation.

Many people have contributed to the ideas I have included in this book. Ron Burke and Tim Hall, my former colleagues at York University, influenced me as I began developing my approach to interviewing. Tom Philbrook has provided valuable counsel and encouragement. Margie Cass has patiently typed and retyped drafts of each chapter. I also owe much to the Personnel Association of Toronto, the College Placement Council, and a number of private corporations in the United States and Canada for whom I have conducted interviewing skills training over the years. My greatest debt, however, is to the thousands of people who have attended my workshops and put my ideas into practice. In working with them I have developed and refined much of the material included in the book.

Finally, I want to thank my wife, Robin, to whom this book is dedicated. A fine writer and editor in her own right, she has encouraged me throughout the writing of this book. She has read the entire manuscript and has made excellent editorial suggestions to assist me in presenting my ideas clearly and succinctly.

# The Fine Art of Interviewing

# 1

## Introduction

Interviewing is an art. It is a delight to watch an effective interviewer, who relaxes the other person and strikes up an almost immediate rapport, conducts a smooth, seemingly effortless and unstructured conversation, and then ends the interview only after having covered all necessary topics and having collected all needed information. Many of us have known people who appear to conduct effective interviews almost by intuition and seem to have the knack to say the right thing at the right time. We are inclined to attribute their success to personality and intuitive feel and therefore conclude that a good interviewer is born not made.

This conclusion, however, is simply not true.

There is much that we do *not* see as we watch the fine art of interviewing. You can be sure that rigorous training in basic principles, countless hours of study and practice, and careful planning have preceded the finished product. We are familiar with many art forms that appear effortless but are grounded in years of training by the artist. Just as the ballet dancer, the professional athlete, and the professional comedian have planned and practiced each individual action we observe in their seemingly effortless performances, successful interviewers have worked very hard to perfect their art. As with any other art form, interviewing must be grounded in sound principles and excellent technique.

Successful interviewing can be systematically taught and learned as a highly developed skill. Unfortunately, however, working people are often expected to learn how to interview through a process of osmosis. Virtually every business person is regularly involved in some form of interviewing on either the giving or the receiving end, but few are really taught how to interview. Any supervisor or manager is expected routinely to conduct interviews. There are selection interviews to be done with job applicants and counseling, performance appraisal, and disciplinary interviews to be done with current employees. Typically, people in supervisory positions are expected to bring a high level of interviewing skill to their jobs, but unfortunately few really possess this skill. The same is true of people who work in personnel departments and are therefore called upon to conduct selection, counseling, disciplinary, and exit interviews. Their training frequently consists of sitting in with another, more experienced employee during a number of interview sessions and then being turned loose on their own. As many of you probably know, this trial-and-error learning can be as frightening and painful as it is ineffective. The main purpose of this book is to provide an alternative to this trial-and-error learning. I will present and illustrate the principles and techniques you must learn to become an effective interviewer.

## THE IMPORTANCE OF INTERVIEWS

Every working person is significantly influenced by interviews throughout his or her association with an employer. The association begins with a selection interview, the most highly trusted and most commonly used device to help an employer choose the best person for the job. Selection decisions represent not only a major financial investment by an employer but also a major personal investment by an individual. The decision of both parties is strongly influenced by the interview.

After a few months on the job, the new employee is likely to take part in a variety of additional interviews. A career planning interview may occur in which long-term plans may be set for the employee's training and professional development and desired progression of jobs within the organization. This interview is clearly of critical importance to the employee's successful and satisfying future with the firm. The employee will also likely participate in some form of performance appraisal interview. This is a discussion between the employee and his or her immediate supervisor in which the employee's past performance is reviewed and evaluated and plans are made to help the employee reach performance goals in the future. Salary increases and promotions may also be discussed in performance appraisal interviews, and these topics add to the importance of the interview both to the supervisor and the employee.

Many employees will participate in a counseling interview or a disciplinary interview during their work careers. Both interviews require a great deal of skill because they occur with employees who need help. These interviews can be highly emotional and very difficult discussions for both parties. The counseling interview is typically initiated by an employee who is experiencing stress from a personal or work-related problem which may be interfering with effective work performance. The disciplinary interview, initiated by the employer, involves a confronting discussion with an employee who has violated an important rule or policy or who has consistently performed below acceptable standards.

Even as they leave an organization, employees are also likely to encounter an interview. Many companies conduct exit interviews to learn why employees leave their jobs. These interviews may identify internal problems which have contributed to employee dissatisfaction and turnover. The exit interview may also involve strong emotions and requires a good deal of skill for the interviewer to get valid, useful information.

All these interviews conducted either by supervisors and managers or by personnel specialists are of major importance to the organization's objective of placing and keeping the right person in the right job. These interviews strongly influence the work life of the average employee. However, the effects of interviews on both the company and the employee are often negative because the interviews are poorly conceived and conducted.

## GAME PLAYING IN THE INTERVIEW

Interviews have always included an element of game playing in which each party tries to outfox the other. Typically a respondent tries to guess what information the interviewer is looking for and then gives the interviewer only that part of the information which is to his or her own advantage, while hiding his or her weaknesses. For example, a job applicant will emphasize the positive points of his or her background and try to avoid discussion of any negative items. In a performance appraisal interview, the employee asked for a self-evaluation will likely emphasize the strengths of recent job performance and overlook the blunders. Meanwhile, the intrepid interviewer tries to break through the respondent's façade, often using trick questions or other devious techniques, to get a look at the real person. As a result, the interview may degenerate into a game in which each party is trying to outguess and trick the other.

It is evident that such game playing is more common in interviews today than it was ten or fifteen years ago. A major reason for this trend is that interviewees are growing more skillful, whereas interviewers are performing at a relatively constant level of efficiency.

We have definitely entered the age of the professional interviewee. While this is true for all the interviews covered in this book, it is especially well illustrated in the selection interview. Anyone who has interviewed recent university graduates applying for a job has probably encountered the well-prepared, smooth applicant who can take control of the selection interview and run it to his or her own advantage. It is common for students to receive coaching and to participate in practice sessions for recruiting interviews. There are even seminars given by professors on how to sell oneself in an interview. In addition, students often take on-campus interviews just for practice. And business magazines have even published articles which give sample questions of recruiters and then suggest good answers. In general, people being interviewed are more sophisticated today than ever before.

I would argue, however, that line managers and personnel specialists who conduct various kinds of interviews have not increased their skill over the past decade. Newly hired employees are reporting the same blunders made by interviewers today that they reported ten years ago. In my years of conducting interviewing workshops, I have seen no marked improvement in the practitioners entering the course. I believe that this lack of expertise is due to the common business practice of assuming that people whose jobs involve much communication can interview effectively with no additional training. To the contrary, interviewing is extremely difficult, highly skilled work which can seldom be mastered through trial and error. I believe strongly that game playing in interviews will diminish as interviewers become more proficient. Skillful interviewers can cut quite quickly through the façade and tricks of a respondent, take control, and conduct effective and efficient interviews.

## CONSEQUENCES OF POOR INTERVIEWING

Interviewing is a highly subjective process. There is a disturbing amount of evidence to indicate that, if two members of an organization interview the same person at different times, the outcome of the interviews will differ. For example, if two managers interview the same applicant for a job, one may recommend hiring the applicant, but the other may not be at all impressed with the person. Similarly, if a troubled employee goes to two different people for counseling, he or she might leave one interview feeling misunderstood and intimidated, while the other interview might lead to excellent problem solving and a viable plan for improvement. Of course, interviewers will almost invariably differ somewhat in their style and in the way they interpret information and make decisions. More than a small degree of inconsistency, however, can create serious problems for an organization.

There are three major problems which result from poor interviewing. They are

1.   Failure to meet interview objectives
2.   Poor public relations and employee relations
3.   Charges of discrimination

Let's deal with each in turn.

**Failure to meet interview objectives.**   An interview is an important business transaction designed to meet specific objectives. If interviewers do not identify the objectives and systematically set out to accomplish them, the interview will likely fail. For example, the wrong applicant may be selected for the job, the employee's weakness will not be discussed and corrected in a performance appraisal interview, or the major problem of a department will not be uncovered in a series of exit interviews. All these failures waste time and money.

**Poor public relations and employee relations.**   As serious as failure to meet objectives is, it may be the least of the poor interviewer's worries. We must consider the interviewee's perception of a poor interview. Untrained or unskilled interviewers are perceived by employees or applicants as being incompetent, arbitrary, or unfair. Applicants who are subjected to amateurish selection interviews form low opinions of the organization doing the hiring. This adds up to a poor image and poor public relations for the organization. Managers who have bungled performance appraisal, career planning, or counseling interviews with their own employees know the costs. Nothing can destroy a superior–subordinate relationship more quickly than an interview on crucial matters (promotion potential, future with the company, nagging work problem) between an employee and a seemingly uncaring or unfair boss. As we proceed through this book, I will demonstrate how you can do your job in the interview and still maintain good relations with the interviewee.

**Charges of discrimination.**   Poor interviewers now run the risk of having their organizations sued for discrimination. Untrained interviewers often base their decisions to hire, promote, or fire someone on intuition or personality. Such highly subjective judgments are open to the challenge of being unfair or discriminatory. This is particularly true for selection interviewing. Title VII of the Civil Rights Act of 1964 prohibits discrimination in employment because of race, color, religion, sex, or national origin. Furthermore, Equal Employment Opportunity Commission guidelines on employment selection procedures of 1978 require that selection tests be demonstrated as predictive of job performance. The government now regards the selection interview as the same as a test. This legislation provides two clear warnings to organizations. First, make sure your selection interviewers are basing their hiring decisions on job-related information, and, second, be able to demonstrate that the selection interviews actually predict how well individuals will perform on the job. Under close scrutiny, many organizations might fail to meet these two criteria.

The possibility of charges of discrimination extends beyond the selection interview. Title VII of the Civil Rights Act also requires that employers keep for six months records pertinent to hiring, promotion, demotion, transfer, lay-off or termination, and rates of pay of employees. Disciplinary, performance appraisal, counseling, and career planning interviews frequently contribute to decisions on all these matters. These interviews must be done carefully so that the decisions are made on the basis of job-related information. If the interviewer can be accused of firing or failing to promote an employee because of a "personality conflict" or intuition, the organization may be open to the charge of discrimination. As I cover each kind of interview in this book, I will discuss ways that interviewers can safeguard against charges of discrimination. Suffice it to say now that skillful interviewers can help the organization to avoid major problems.

## THE ART OF INTERVIEWING

As I have said, interviewing is a skill which can be taught. There are two basic ingredients of a successful interview: *content* and *conducting*. Content refers to the topics and questions covered in the interview; conducting refers to the *way* in which the interviewer covers the content (e.g., how to phrase questions, when to listen and when to speak, how to guide the conversation subtly, and how to relax respondents and get them to volunteer needed information). The interviewer must cover the appropriate topics and ask the right questions (content) to be successful. In addition, the interviewer must conduct the interview properly by using a variety of communication skills to open up the respondent and draw out the information being sought.

If either ingredient is lacking, the interviewer will fail. For example, I have known recruiters who conducted selection interviews very smoothly, establishing rapport and probing deftly while maintaining an easy conversational tone, but they unfortunately asked irrelevant questions and covered the wrong topics, so they were unable to evaluate the applicant's potential to do the job. This is frequently the downfall of supervisors or line managers who are excellent communicators but have little experience in systematically preparing the content of an interview.

Other people may plan the interview very carefully, listing topics and even questions to be covered, but they conduct the interview poorly. They fail to establish rapport, or they ask questions in a stilted, mechanical way which unsettles respondents and does not allow them to relax and open up. In this case, the interview may degenerate to the point that it sounds like an interrogation based on an orally administered questionnaire.

## CONTENT

Most interviews are weak in content. The interviewer is certainly more likely to fail because of poor content than because of the interviewer's weakness in conducting the interview. This is true simply because people do not take the time or have the knowledge necessary to plan an interview systematically.

Throughout this book, I will introduce each major type of interview with a developmental sequence shown in Table 1.1. You will find it simple and effective. Once you have identified the type of interview to be created, you should next turn to objectives. Every type of interview covered in this book has several objec-

## TABLE 1.1
### Sequence for Planning Interview Content

| Developmental sequence | Illustration |
|---|---|
| I. Type of interview | Selection interview |
| II. Objectives | A. Collect information to assess<br>   1. Potential to perform the job<br>   2. Willingness to perform the job<br>B. Provide information about job and company<br>C. Check personal chemistry |
| III. Approach and style | A. Semistructured<br>B. Tailored to the specific job<br>C. Flexible and conversational |
| IV. Format | A. Establish rapport<br>B. Set agenda<br>C. Collect information about applicant<br>D. Discuss job and company more thoroughly<br>E. Invite applicant's questions<br>F. Terminate interview |
| V. Topics | A. Previous work experience in specific job functions<br>B. Previous training and education<br>C. Hints of career plans and interests<br>D. Explanation of the job and company benefits |

tives. It is obvious that, to design an effective interview, you must first know the objectives to be achieved. Next, you must consider the general approach and style of the interview. Should it be relaxed and conversational, or should it be more formal? Should the interview be highly structured with a long list of questions to be asked, or should it have no structure at all, allowing the interviewer the freedom of investigating any topic that seems relevant? As we proceed through the book, I will argue that the most effective interview should be semistructured; that is, topics have been identified, but there is flexibility for you to cover the topics as you wish with various communication skills and techniques.

Next, a format must be considered. Generally, interviewers

waste time by repeating themselves or drifting off topic. A format that coincides with the objectives of the interview will promote efficiency. The final step in planning an interview is to make a list of topics and in some cases a few questions to be covered faithfully during the interview. In summary, if you cover a planned list of topics and work through the format according to the prescribed style, you will have achieved your objectives, and the interview will be successful.

Many managers or personnel specialists faced with the chore of conducting an interview fail to plan its content properly because they do not work systematically through this sequence. Many jump from step I to step V as outlined in Table 1.1. "Well," they say, "I have to see those applicants for the administrative assistant job. What shall I ask them?" or "I've got to do a performance appraisal interview with Jones next week. What can I say about how she has been doing?"

Systematic planning for an interview is essential. I wish to emphasize, however, that a well-planned and well-conducted interview should appear to have very little structure to the respondent. Planned need not translate into rigid or awkward. The key here is flexibility. A semistructured approach allows needed flexibility for you to vary questioning techniques, phrasing, and style. This flexibility will allow you the freedom to make the interview appear like a smooth, unstructured conversation. This is what makes interviewing a fine art.

## CONDUCTING

This brings us to the communication skills and techniques needed to transform a carefully planned, semistructured interview into an apparently unplanned, unstructured conversation. This is truly an art which must be developed through practice. Like any other skill, conducting an interview is based on fundamentals which, if learned and practiced, will lead to success.

These fundamentals, outlined in Table 1.2, will be present in all six types of interviews discussed in this book. They will become clearer as I apply them to each specific type of interview, but it is useful to describe them in general terms now. Let's take them in order.

# TABLE 1.2
## Principles for Conducting Interviews

| Sequence | | Illustration |
|---|---|---|
| I. Initiate | State the purpose of the interview and get the interviewee talking | Open-ended questions |
| II. Listen | Listen actively and store topics to be pursued | Listen for your agenda items |
| III. Focus | Direct the interviewee's attention to topics he or she raised which you want to probe further | "You mentioned. . ." "I'm particularly interested in. . ." |
| IV. Probe | Probe into relevant topics raised by the interviewee and pursue additional topics you have planned to cover | Non-directive techniques Specific questions re: how, why, how well |
| V. Use | Use the information you have gained during the interview to meet your interview objectives | Conclude the interview appropriately, incorporating one or more of the following: evaluation, plans, and decisions |

**Initiate.** It's your interview, and you have the responsibility of establishing and maintaining control from the beginning. It is helpful to summarize the purpose of the interview and to set an agenda. Then move into the body of the interview by asking a general, open-ended question. An example of such a question in a selection interview is, "I noticed on your resumé that your most recent job was in sales. Will you please summarize your major responsibilities in that job?" In a performance appraisal interview, an early question might be, "What have you achieved in the past six months that you have found particularly satisfying?" The objective here is to get the respondent talking about some topics you want to address in the interview.

**Listen.** I cannot overemphasize the importance of active listening in an interview. It requires careful preparation before the interview and good concentration during the interview. Preparation is necessary to still that little voice which interviewers often hear in their minds when the other person is talking. The little voice says, "What am I going to say when he (or she) stops talking?" If you are thoroughly prepared and have a list of topics you want to cover in the interview, active listening is simply hearing and remembering important subjects that you wish to pursue later. Some of these subjects may be on your prepared list of topics, and others may not. While active listening is particularly important in the early stages of an interview, it is, of course, essential throughout the entire interview.

**Focus.**    In the interview you wish to cover your topics as efficiently as possible. It is therefore your responsibility to direct the respondent's attention to what you want to talk about. You can do so with open-ended questions, as I have already said. Another technique is to refer to something the respondent has already said and then pursue that topic. For example, you might say, "You mentioned that your job involved maintaining good relationships with customers. Can you tell me how you approached that part of your job?" Another example is, "You raised a very interesting point which I'd like to pursue. What steps have you taken to create this spirit of teamwork in your group?" These comments and questions not only focus the discussion, but they also add to the conversational tone of the interview. A useful technique in interviewing is to try to get respondents to raise some of *your* topics. Then when you follow up on their (your) topics, the interview appears more like an unplanned, unstructured conversation.

**Probe.**    You have to probe and pry (in a friendly and professional manner) into what the respondent says until you learn what you are seeking in the interview. Many interviewers fail because they take the first answer and only afterward realize that they did not learn enough. This is the time to probe thoroughly the topics raised by the respondent, and then introduce and probe into additional topics you wish to cover.

**Use.**    Every interview has a purpose beyond information gathering. The information must be used to evaluate, plan, and make decisions. In a selection interview, you must evaluate the applicant's potential to perform the job. In a counseling interview, problem definition should be followed by problem solving and goal setting. In an appraisal interview, the employee and supervisor may jointly evaluate the employee's past performance and make mutual plans for changes in the future. Having the information's use in mind during the interview not only helps you probe until you feel you have sufficient information but also helps you go ahead and make use of the information during or immediately after the interview. You have not completed your responsibility as an interviewer until you have converted the raw information collected in the interview into the appropriate evaluation, plan, or decision.

## INTERVIEWING SKILLS AND TECHNIQUES

Throughout the interview it is imperative that the interviewer keep the channels of communication wide open. A number of techniques promote maximal information flow between the two parties by encouraging the respondent to open up and talk in a relatively unguarded way; these techniques also help promote a smooth, conversational tone.

I shall discuss these techniques in general terms here. Specific illustrations of each will appear many times in interview transcripts throughout the book. These techniques can be identified and practiced, but they cannot be programmed. Only experience will help you develop the art of choosing among them—of knowing when to ask a specific question, when to nod your head, when to reflect a feeling, and when to say nothing.

Please note that overindulgence in any of these is bad. Each form of response should be used sparingly as it seems to fit.

### NONDIRECTIVE TECHNIQUES

1. *Pause.* The most purely nondirective technique is the pause, where the interviewer simply says nothing. A ten-second pause puts great pressure on the respondent to say more. While

the pause should be used sparingly, interviewers should avoid feeling compelled to leap forward and fill the air with words during occasional lapses in the conversation. Wait it out a few seconds.

2. *Head nod; um huh.* A large body of research demonstrates that, if the interviewer simply nods his or her head or says "um huh," the respondent will be encouraged to say more. This is just a subtle way of showing respondents that you are paying attention and taking in what they are saying.

3. *Reflecting ideas.* Here the interviewer paraphrases what the other party has said. This response usually leads to further comments by the interviewee.

RESPONDENT:    ". . . and I also filled in for the foreman when he was tied up."

INTERVIEWER:    "So you did occasionally have some supervisory responsibility on this job."

RESPONDENT:    "Oh yes, the boss was usually away a couple of days each month and I would handle the scheduling of the work for five men and also . . ."

4. *Reflecting feelings.* Every spoken thought has two components: an idea and the speaker's feelings about that idea. Often the feeling component is indifference, but in some interviews very strong feelings can be expressed. It is crucial that the interviewer detect and acknowledge the respondent's feelings rather than trying to ignore them. This is particularly important in counseling, exit, and performance appraisal interviews. The emotions of the respondent must be put on the table and dealt with as a part of solving problems and making changes.

RESPONDENT:    "I figured that I couldn't do their work and mine, so I had to stop helping out the other supervisors as much as I used to."

INTERVIEWER:    "You don't sound very happy about that decision."

RESPONDENT:    "I'm not, but I had to cut down. I was spreading myself too thin."

INTERVIEWER:    "I guess you felt practically at your wit's end."

RESPONDENT:    "Well, I just couldn't think of anything else to do."

INTERVIEWER:    "You sound pretty frustrated about the whole situation."

RESPONDENT:    "I am. Hell, those guys won't even talk to me anymore."

INTERVIEWER:    "I doubt if that's the reaction you wanted."

RESPONDENT:    "Well no, not at all."

INTERVIEWER:    "Let's see if we can come up with some other ideas of how to handle this predicament."

In this case the respondent is feeling a good deal of pain and frustration. It is best to acknowledge and deal with these feelings first and then turn to a rational discussion of alternatives.

5. *Summarizing.* Summarizing has many uses. It is a way for you to check your understanding of what the respondent has said, and it also serves as a stimulus for the respondent to add more.

INTERVIEWER:    "So in essence, you are having difficulty adjusting to this new team member."

RESPONDENT:    "Well, that's part of it, but the addition of that person has also altered my job. You see, I used to have sole responsibility . . ."

By summarizing in the illustration given, the interviewer also identified a major theme in the discussion that can be referred to later to focus the conversation.

Summarizing is also useful in making smooth transitions from one topic to another. Notice how the lack of transition in the following example makes the interview rather stilted and awkward.

RESPONDENT:    ". . . and in addition to my major responsibility of supervising the clerks and scheduling their work, I was also charged with controlling the budget."

INTERVIEWER:    "Um huh, O.K. How much did you get involved in the technical detail of your clerks' work?"

The transition in the interview from the supervisory elements of the applicant's job to the technical responsibilities is more smooth with a summary.

RESPONDENT:   ". . . and in addition to my major responsibility of supervising the clerks and scheduling their work, I was also charged with controlling the budget."

INTERVIEWER:   "So your primary supervisory responsibilities were to plan the work day, allocate work loads to your various clerks, and check their work on a daily basis. You also kept the department within budget. Is that correct?"

RESPONDENT:   "Yes."

INTERVIEWER:   "Well, I think I understand that part of your former work quite well. Now I'd like to turn to another topic. To what extent did you get involved in the actual technical detail of your clerks' work?"

I list the nondirective techniques first because they stimulate the respondents to say more without actually asking them a question. They contribute to the conversational tone of the interview and give it the appearance of being unstructured and unplanned. Too much reliance on the direct question can turn the interview into an interrogation with the emerging sequence of question, answer, question, answer, question, answer. I recommend therefore that you make good use of these nondirective techniques when conducting interviews.

## DIRECTIVE TECHNIQUES

1. *Open-ended question.* An open-ended question is simply one which cannot be answered yes or no. While these questions are useful throughout the interview, they are particularly appropriate in the early stages to get the respondent talking. In a selection interview, an early open-ended question might be, "What were the major responsibilities of your most recent job?" An exit interview might include an early question such as, "What were the major factors you considered in your decision to leave us?"

2. *Specific probe.* This type of question is used to focus on a particular topic. It often accompanies a restatement of what the respondent has just said, as shown now.

RESPONDENT:   "I've always had the ability to get my employees to extend themselves and work hard for me."

INTERVIEWER:   "So you feel you've had success at motivating people. What specific steps do you take to promote this kind of motivation in your employees?"

One very common probe is to ask for elaboration or clarification. For example, if you have asked a well-considered open-ended question and you received only five words in return, you may ask the respondent to elaborate, as in the following example from a performance appraisal interview.

SUPERVISOR:   "So, as you look over the last year's work, how would you rate your own performance?"

EMPLOYEE:   "I think I'm doing great."

SUPERVISOR:   "I'm glad to hear that you feel that way. Could you elaborate for me a bit?"

Or

SUPERVISOR:   "I'm pleased to hear that. What accomplishments in particular have made you feel that way?"

All the responses discussed keep the channels of communication wide open and stimulate the respondent to talk. As I have already said, heavy use of any one of those techniques will lead to a noticeable and distracting pattern in the interview and should therefore be avoided. Knowledge of each technique, together with practice and experience, will contribute to more efficient and conversational interviews.

## THE INTERVIEWER

One critical contributor to the success of the interview which is frequently overlooked is the manner of the interviewer. Interviewers need to win the confidence and trust of the person being interviewed, and doing so is unlikely when the interviewer speaks in a monotone, sits in a slumped position with a bored expression on his or her face, and stares into space. Interviewers need to be more aware of their eye contact, voice, and posture. A rather peculiar characteristic of North American culture is reflected in how seldom people look one another in the eye during conversation. I encourage interviewers to make frequent eye contact with the respondent. Of course, this should not be carried to excess as in a staring contest, but eye contact builds excellent rapport.

Interviewers should also be aware of their posture and the inflection of their voices. This is especially true for recruiters who interview frequently and who, as representatives of the firm, are trying to attract applicants. A rule of thumb is to let your interest and excitement come through in your voice and posture—lean forward and let your voice rise. Too many interviewers unintentionally lapse into a monotone which may bore the respondent. Listen to yourself and show what you feel. You'll be surprised at how much more positively the person you are interviewing will react.

## THE PERSONAL TOUCH

As as interviewer, you are a personal link between the applicant or employee being interviewed and the organization you represent. To the applicant or employee, that organization and its policies and procedures may appear quite formal and imposing. For example, the job applicant may see the organization mainly as a printed brochure and a confusing series of tests and hurdles between applying for the job and possible employment. As the recruiter, you can welcome the applicant sincerely and explain the hiring procedures to remove his or her confusion and apprehension. Similarly, an employee who knows that his or her work is suffering as a result of wrestling with a difficult problem may perceive the company as insensitive and uncaring. As a supervisor conducting a counseling or performance appraisal interview, however, you can demonstrate that you want to help the employee improve his or her performance. In short, as an interviewer you have a responsibility to treat interviewees with understanding and respect.

Now I want to be very clear about this point. I'm not proposing that you shirk your other responsibilities as a manager or personnel specialist and be "soft" on interviewees. I do wish to emphasize, however, that the art of interviewing is to meet your goals in the interview but still maintain positive employee relations. Furthermore, if you gain good rapport with your interviewee and are perceived as interested and supportive, you will find it easier to meet your objectives in the interview. I will stress throughout this book the techniques you can use to conduct the interview as a relatively informal conversation and yet still accomplish everything you set out to achieve in the interview.

## THE PLAN OF THIS BOOK

In the next six chapters, I will cover six common types of interviews conducted by personnel specialists as well as supervisors and managers. I have tried to present each in a very practical way so that you can take the material into the context of your own jobs and use it immediately. You will find that there are clear relationships among the six interviews included in this book. For example, effective selection interviews will increase the chances of successful performance appraisal and career planning interviews. Similarly, in organizations where selection, performance appraisal, and counseling interviews are done poorly or too seldom, there may be a corresponding increase in disciplinary and exit interviews. In short, as a successful manager or personnel specialist, you need to be prepared to conduct a variety of interviews well. Helping you learn to do so is the primary purpose of this book. In each chapter I will present an approach and specific guidelines for the interview being covered. I will also present illustrations in the body of each chapter, and in some cases interview transcripts.

# 2

# Selection Interviewing

The selection interview is a discussion between an individual applying for a job and a representative of the organization that is hiring. I am using the term "selection interview" in the generic sense. Therefore, it may refer to any one of a series of interviews which are used to identify the best applicant for the job. The term refers to the first contact between the two parties, sometimes called the recruiting, campus, or screening interview, and it also refers to the final interview before hiring, which usually occurs between applicants and their potential immediate supervisor. Applicants may be from outside the organization, or they may be internal applicants who are hoping to change jobs within the organization.

The selection interview is by far the most common of all the interviews to be discussed in this book. While counseling or career planning interviews may be relatively rare in some organizations, there is ample evidence that virtually all organizations use the interview for selection purposes. It may also be argued that the selection interview is the most important of all interviews, because the decision to hire an individual represents a major investment by the organization. Furthermore, the interview is the most widely used and highly trusted selection device available to the personnel specialist or supervisor. It is the most personal step in the selection procedure. You may learn *what* an applicant has done on paper, but the interview enables you to learn *how*, *why*, and *how well*. Therefore, in spite of how good applicants look on paper—test scores, resumés, application forms, letters of recommendation—very nearly all are interviewed by the personnel department and by the applicant's potential boss.

## *OBJECTIVES*

A major reason for the selection interview's popularity is that it meets several objectives of both the interviewer and the applicant. Among the interviewer's goals are

1. Gathering information about applicants that will assist in the prediction of future performance: how well they will perform and how long they will remain in the organization.
2. Informing applicants about the job and organization and attracting them to the organization.
3. Determining whether the "personal chemistry" is good between applicants and the people with whom they will be working.

Applicants' goals include

1. Presenting themselves favorably and selling themselves to the interviewer.
2. Collecting information about the job and organization so they can make an informed decision about accepting employment.
3. Testing personal chemistry.

A glance at these objectives reveals that the first two of each list may be in conflict, hence making interviewing quite difficult. In objective 1 interviewers are seeking good, predictive information, whereas applicants are trying to sell themselves and look their best. Often the information sent is not that which is needed. This is particularly true as applicants become more skillful at taking interviews. Applicants also employ evasive tactics such as saying "that's a very good question" and then not answering it. This game playing makes effective selection interviewing very difficult, especially for interviewers who have received no formal guidance.

Another point about these objectives is that a two-way selection decision is being made. Not only is the interviewer selecting the applicant, but the applicant is selecting the organization. Therefore, in objective 2, applicants may have to sift through the interviewer's presentation of the position and company to decide if this is the kind of job they really want. These potentially antagonistic positions make good information flow difficult.

Finally, these objectives place interviewers in a rather divided position. In objective 1 they are scrutinizing applicants in an attempt to learn if the applicants show the potential to do the job, but in objective 2 they are also trying to attract applicants to the firm. Interviewers must sometimes ask difficult questions to allow applicants an opportunity to show their true potential. They must do so in a way that does not place too much stress on applicants, however, because they want all applicants to leave the interview with a favorable impression of their organization. This dual purpose of scrutinizing and attracting the applicant requires a high level of skill from interviewers.

All these objectives must be met if any selection interview is to be effective, although some may be emphasized more than others. For example, a first interview on campus may stress attracting applicants and testing personal chemistry more than a detailed examination of the applicants' potential to perform a specific job; a final interview conducted by a potential supervisor may stress scrutinizing the applicant and testing personal chemistry more than attracting the applicant. But, generally, all objectives are given some attention in all selection interviews, and the interviews need to be planned accordingly.

The selection interview definitely fulfills some of these objectives better than others. It allows both parties to test personal chemistry and provides an excellent format in which both the interviewer and the applicant can give and receive useful information. As a predictive device which contributes to the selection decision, however, the interview has had only limited success. In short, the assessment which an interviewer makes of an applicant is very poorly related to that applicant's actual job performance after being hired.

## CORRECTING THE SELECTION
## INTERVIEW'S WEAKNESSES

I believe in the selection interview. It can be an effective tool for meeting its primary objective—choosing the best applicant for the job. But, as commonly practiced, the selection interview often does not meet this objective. The failure of the interview to predict future performance can typically be traced to how the interview was designed and conducted. In this chapter we will focus on the two essential ingredients of an effective interview: *content* and *conducting*. As noted in Chapter 1, content refers to the topics covered in the interview and the questions that are asked. Conducting refers to the *way* in which the interviewer covers the content, for example, guiding the conversation, phrasing the questions, and getting applicants to volunteer the information needed for a valid selection decision.

We will begin with the content of the selection interview—how it is planned and designed. This is its Achilles heel. Most people, be they personnel specialists or supervisors, communicate relatively well, but they may know very little about what topics should be covered in the selection interview and, in the context of EEO, what topics should be avoided. We will cover four major weaknesses of the interview, listed in Table 2.1, and ways in which these weaknesses can be minimized, summarized in Table 2.2.

The interview is probably the most thoroughly researched and yet most poorly applied of all available selection devices. Beginning as early as 1915[1], several hundred studies have uncovered and focused on the frailties of the selection interview. The conclusions of over sixty years of research have been resoundingly negative. Major reviews[2] have stated and restated that the selection interview has low reliability and low predictive validity. By *low reliability* I mean that *two interviewers do not agree in their assessments of the same applicant*. By *low predictive validity* I

### TABLE 2.1

### Weaknesses of the Selection Interview

I. Planning Is Poor
  A. Interviewers do not know their objectives
  B. Interviewers do not plan and structure the interview
  C. Interviewers do not know the job for which the candidate is applying
II. Approach Is Psychiatric
  A. Interviewer assumes the role of amateur psychiatrist
  B. Applicant is judged on inappropriate criteria
III. Interviewers Are Human Beings
  A. Personal attitudes and stereotypes abound
  B. First-impression bias and jumping to conclusions are apparent
  C. Interviewer forgets
IV. Interviewers Violate EEO Guidelines
  A. Interviewer raises prohibited topics
  B. Evaluation is based on irrelevant information

### TABLE 2.2

### Improving the Interview as a Selection Device

I. Planning Properly
  A. Know your objectives
  B. Plan an interview format to meet those objectives
  C. Know as much as possible about the job to be filled
II. Evaluate Applicants' Potential to Perform
  A. Evaluate applicants in terms of potential to perform job-related functions
  B. Evaluate applicants' willingness to work for your organization
III. Build a Better Interview
  A. Whenever possible, tailor the interview to a specific job
  B. Systematically cover job-related topics in the interview
  C. Record your evaluations and supportive documentation
IV. Make Your Interviews Meet EEO Standards
  A. Tailor the interview to the job
  B. Systematically cover job-related topics
  C. Evaluate applicants in job-related terms
  D. Retain evaluations and supportive documentation

mean that *there is little or no statistical relationship between an interviewer's assessment of an applicant's potential to succeed in a job and that applicant's actual performance after being hired.*

There are several major reasons for the interview's failure, and many of the sources of failure are under the control of the interviewer. This is encouraging, because it means that an awareness of the pitfalls of the selection interview can help us to develop more effective interviews. Let's take a look at some major pitfalls.

## POOR VERSUS PROPER PLANNING

Many selection interviews are simply not carefully planned. With their hectic schedules, many personnel specialists find themselves facing an applicant on a university campus or in their own offices before they have had much time to think carefully about the interview they are about to conduct. Because they see job applicants infrequently, supervisors or line managers may also take little time to plan a selection interview.

The interview is likely to fail if interviewers do not know their objectives and do not develop a plan to meet those objectives. Lack of planning usually leads to a relatively unstructured interview in which whatever comes up automatically becomes the content of today's interview. Lack of structure creates problems because the less structured the interview is, the less reliable it will be. That is, two interviewers are less likely to agree in their assessments of an applicant if they enter the interview with different objectives and approaches. Furthermore, since the major objective of a selection interview is to choose the person most qualified to do the job, the *interviewer's* knowledge of the job is crucial. The less you know about the job to be filled, the less qualified you are to examine an applicant's potential to perform that job successfully and to make a valid selection decision about that applicant.

Developing a general plan for the selection interview is relatively straightforward. Interviewers must know their objectives and then design the interview so that each objective is met. Furthermore, since the main objective is to assess each applicant's potential to do the job, interviewers must know as much about the job in question as possible. I recommend a *semistructured* approach in which the main components of the interview are laid out in order but which still allows interviewers to pursue topics in a flexible manner. Here is my suggestion for the overall format of the selection interview.

1. *Establish rapport.* Begin by introducing yourself and stating the job and organization you are representing. Next, welcoming applicants warmly and making small talk will help to set them at ease. A note on small talk. Avoid picking a topic randomly because it will appear forced. Study the resumé or application blank beforehand and look for something in common: a school, a part of the country, a person, a hobby, for example. This gives you a good place to begin your small talk.

2. *Set the agenda.* Explain briefly the objectives of the interview and provide a short outline. This is useful for two reasons. First, it can help to relax applicants by letting them know what's coming. Second, it puts the interviewer in control of the interview by providing a road map to be followed. I recommend that the outline be a paraphrase of the next three steps, for example, "In the next half hour I'll be asking you several questions about yourself and your past work and educational experience. Then I'll explain the specific position you're applying for in more detail and describe our organization to you. Later on in the interview I'll give you a chance to ask any questions which I may not have already answered. I'll be jotting down a note from time to time as we go along."

Setting the agenda helps interviewers fend off attempts by well-rehearsed or game-playing applicants who attempt to change the subject or jump into another stage of the interview when they feel challenged or want to take control of the interview themselves. For example, if you are probing an applicant's work experience and he or she asks you to describe training and career development opportunities, having set the agenda makes it easier for you to say, "I want to be sure all your questions and concerns are addressed, but could we hold off until later to cover that area? Please help me to remember to answer your question then."

3. *Gather information.* Here is where the primary objectives of both the interviewer and the applicant are met. This is the detailed discussion of the applicant's past which helps the interviewer determine whether the applicant is suitable for the job. It is in this section that we answer the two questions, *"Can* the applicant do the job?" and *"Will* the applicant do the job?" I will cover this component of the interview in more detail in a later section of this chapter.

4. *Describe the job and organization.* Many interviewers describe the job briefly early in the interview, and often this is done in a recruiting ad, but a detailed description of duties is best saved until this stage of the interview. By describing the job *before* stage 3, the interviewer may inadvertently be coaching applicants on how they should appear today—how they can look as good as possible.

5. *Answer questions and allow the applicant to add information.* This stage is directed toward applicants' objectives—to gather information about the job and company and to sell themselves. They should be given the opportunity to do both.

6. *Terminate.* Simply thanking applicants for their time and telling them what will happen next (e.g., "We'll be interviewing for the next two weeks and we'll telephone you with our decision within the next three weeks") is an honest and comfortable way to end the interview.


## THE INTERVIEW
## AS AMATEUR PSYCHIATRY

Probably the greatest weakness in the selection interview is the way in which we human beings evaluate applicants. All too often interviewers try to assess an applicant's basic character in half an hour. Judgments are made about the applicant's personality characteristics as well as his or her skills and knowledge. Although there is no way to eliminate subjectivity from the selection interview, these evaluations of the applicant are often more subjective than they need be. Let's examine more closely the evaluation process often used by interviewers.

Information is collected during the interview to answer two fundamental questions:

1.  Will the applicant perform the job?
2.  Can the applicant perform the job?

The assessment of the applicant's willingness to perform the job deals with interest and intention, which are very difficult to judge. As interviewers you must learn whether the applicant really wants to work for your organization, to pursue a particular career, and to accept an available job. I will deal with how you can make these assessments later in the chapter.

Determining whether an applicant *can* perform the job is also a difficult task. Here you must concentrate on what applicants have done or learned in the past and assess whether that experience and knowledge will enable them to perform successfully in the job to be filled.

All interviewers have at their disposal the same basic sources of information which relate to whether the applicant *can do the job.* The information is behavior, either that which is reported from the past or that which takes place during the interview. These sources are

1.  Previous work or nonwork experience
2.  Previous education and training
3.  Current behavior

These sources of information are shown in the left-hand column of Figure 2.1. What interviewers do with this information is a common human tendency which has been institutionalized in selection interviewing. A translation is made from what applicants have done and are doing to what kind of people they are, in terms of basic traits and characteristics. Shortly after we meet another person, we begin categorizing and labeling him or her in terms of traits such as initiative, aggressiveness, personality, intelligence, maturity. These traits are generally poorly defined. What may be initiative to one interviewer may be considered aggressiveness by another. Furthermore, traits are not observed directly. We do not

# FIGURE 2.1
## The Evaluation Process

**BEHAVIOR**

What the Applicant Will Do After Hired

Sample Job    Entry-level accountant in a Financial
              Controls Department.

1. Preparing journal vouchers in a precise and orderly manner for a variety of accounting data.

2. Keeping good working files on areas of accounting responsibility.

3. Checking receipts and other tickets against source data in a fast and accurate manner.

4. Looking for variances in accounting data so as to make needed adjustments.

5. Meeting cycle cut-offs without undue strain or panic effort.

6. Condensing and presenting accounting data in written or oral form to managers.

7. Using time effeciently by setting priorities, laying out and planning tasks, and following instructions and procedures.

8. Exchanging information with others inside and outside the department in a timely, tactful, and precise manner.

9. Improving the accounting system by regularly reviewing procedures and methods of formatting in an effort to find better ways of handling accounting data.

**TRAITS**

What Applicant Is

1. Maturity
2. Intelligence
3. Initiative
4. Aggressiveness
5. Personality
6. Confidence
7. Anxious
8. Good judgment
9. Related experience
10. Self starter

TRANSLATION
- - - - - - ▲

**BEHAVIOR**

What Applicant Has
Done or Is Doing

1. Previous work and nonwork experience
2. Previous training and education
3. Current behavior

TRANSLATION
- - - - - - ▲

THE PROPOSED ROUTE

see initiative. What we do see is behavior from which we *infer* or conclude the underlying trait that we label initiative. In short, when we evaluate applicants in terms of traits, we translate from behavior, which is observable and relatively clearly defined, to unobservable, poorly defined traits.

Many interview guides list a host of traits on which the applicant is to be rated. It is clear that a great deal of subjectivity is introduced during this translation step, and consequently bias can influence the ratings strongly. Much of the unreliability of selection interviews stems from this translation in the evaluation process. Two interviewers may hear an applicant describe a previous work incident, and one may infer a positive trait like initiative, while the other may translate it into something more negative like aggressiveness or pushiness. Simply put, this evaluation scheme puts interviewers in the realm of the unseen and undefined—they act as amateur psychiatrists, judging the basic character of the applicants. Most interviewers are not trained to make these kinds of assessments, nor are they comfortable trying to do so.

Now let's move to the right-hand column of Figure 2.1. Any selection decision is at least implicitly a prediction of future performance.[3] When interviewers pass applicants in the interview and send them on to testing, another interview, or the job, they are at least implicitly predicting that these applicants will perform at an acceptable level in a given job. The predicted behavior can be broken down into specific performance factors such as those in Figure 2.1. Therefore, another translation occurs. A translation is made from a set of traits to probable performance of such an individual. For example, the interviewer concludes that applicants judged as mature because they worked their way through college will work well with little supervision. This translation process becomes even more ambiguous when a third person reviews the interview rating sheet and translates from the middle column to the right-hand column.

The evaluation process in Figure 2.1 can be summarized in the following steps:

1. Collect information about past and present behavior.
2. Translate into poorly defined, inferred traits.
3. Translate into expectations of how the applicant will perform the job.

## SUBJECTIVITY IN EVALUATING
## APPLICANTS' POTENTIAL
## TO PERFORM

There is certainly no way to eliminate subjectivity from interviews, but it can be reduced. Since each of the two translation steps goes from measurable behaviors to inferred traits, it seems reasonable to eliminate the translations. This means eliminating the middle column and simply following the solid arrow in Figure 2.1, from behavior to behavior. Hence, the interviewer uses behavior—past and present—to predict future job performance. Now a point of clarification is needed here. I am not saying that what a person is, in terms of traits, does not influence job performance. I am saying that a concerted effort to assess an applicant's traits is *not necessary* to make a selection decision. The middle column in Figure 2.1 is unnecessary. In practice, assessments in the middle column happen automatically because of the human tendency to jump to conclusions and judge the character of others. These assessments meet the third objective of the selection interview, namely, testing personal chemistry. But an interview that merely tests personal chemistry is very likely to fail as a selection device. Assessing traits will not meet the first objective of gathering information to predict future job performance. This objective can best be met by assessing previous behavior to predict future behavior, shown in Figure 2.1 as the proposed route. Designing and conducting selection interviews so that prediction is made from behavior to behavior is the secret of reliable and valid interviews. We'll see how this can be done shortly. First, however, we will consider another major problem in selection interviewing.

### INTERVIEWERS' BIAS

We all like to think of ourselves as good judges of character, and many of us are. But we each judge character in different ways with reference to different standards, and this spells unreliability. There is no escaping the conclusion that the primary problem with selection interviews is the interviewer. The interviewer is a human being and is therefore susceptible to a number of influences which bias judgments about an applicant and therefore undermine the interview's reliability and predictive validity.

The attitudes and background of interviewers contribute to low reliability by affecting the interviewers' interpretation of what applicants say and their subsequent evaluation of the applicant.[4] It is known that interviewers have a relatively well-defined stereotype of the ideal applicant. Furthermore, those stereotypes of ideal applicants for the same job may differ among interviewers, and the information to which interviewers attend in applicants differs according to the person who conducts the interviews.[5] In short, interviewers may enter the interview with systematic biases which cause them to evaluate the same candidate differently.

These biases are complicated further by the human tendency to jump to conclusions. Several studies[6] have indicated that the interviewer makes a global evaluation of a candidate very early in the interview—as early as the first four minutes. A major problem with these initial impressions is that they are often based on information that has questionable relevance to job performance (e.g., dress, firmness of handshake, hair style). This research suggests that after interviewers have formed an initial impression they selectively seek out and perceive information which is consistent with the initial impression. This selective perception is most likely to occur in an unstructured interview. Forgetting is another important source of error in interviews.[7] Interviewers simply forget much of what they hear. Furthermore, if two interviewers remember *different* information about an applicant, their evaluations of that applicant can differ. *The greatest tragedy in interviewing is the tendency of human beings to distort, ignore, forget, or otherwise waste important information.*

## BUILDING A BETTER INTERVIEW

To remedy this tragic situation, we can change either the interviewer or the interview. As long as people conduct interviews, the problems of selective perception, jumping to conclusions, forgetting, and other forms of bias will persist. Therefore, the more fruitful alternative is to create an interview which minimizes the

effects of human frailties. In short, we must build a better interview.

To do this, we must design an interview for a specific job or
job family and assess applicants in terms of the potential they
show to perform on the job. This puts emphasis on the right-hand
column in Figure 2.1. We already know that reliability increases
when the interview is structured and when the interviewer has
knowledge about the job to be filled. Given this information, we
are more likely to succeed if we prepare and conduct interviews
which are tailored to the job in question. This approach leads to a
different interview with a somewhat different focus for each job to
be filled. In a tailored interview, the applicant's previous work
and nonwork experience, training and education, and current
behavior in the interview are examined. But with a tailored approach we do not fall prey to the amateur psychiatry discussed in
the previous section. The psychiatric approach involves the
assessment of the applicant against the criterion in the middle column of Figure 2.1: "What kind of person is this? What are his or
her basic personality characteristics?" The tailored interview includes a fundamentally different criterion, in the right-hand column of Figure 2.1. It is, "On the basis of what the applicants are
saying and doing, can they perform these nine functions required
of the job? How will her previous experience help her do these
aspects of the job? Has he had any training and education which
he can apply in this job?"

## DESIGNING A TAILORED INTERVIEW

How do we go about designing and conducting tailored interviews? I suggest the following steps. It should be emphasized that
these guidelines are intended to produce only a part of the entire
selection interview, that part which collects information on which
the selection decision is based. This is phase 3 of the overall interview format described earlier.

**Step 1: Start with the job.**    Too often when line managers or
personnel specialists are planning an interview, they think in
terms of the kind of person they want or the qualities of the suc-

cessful applicant. This is not wrong; it's simply premature. The first thought should be about the job to be filled. To select someone with the interview, you must know your objective—job performance. Therefore, you should start with the job by conducting a job analysis and listing major areas of responsibility which, taken together, make up the job. These major areas of responsibility are called "performance factors." The nine performance factors that appear in the right-hand column of Figure 2.1 are restated here. Let's have a closer look at them.

### SAMPLE JOB: ENTRY-LEVEL ACCOUNTANT IN FINANCIAL CONTROLS DEPARTMENT

1. Preparing journal vouchers in a precise and orderly manner for a variety of accounting data.
2. Keeping good working files on areas of accounting responsibility.
3. Checking receipts and other tickets against source data in a fast and accurate manner.
4. Looking for variances in accounting data so as to make needed adjustments.
5. Meeting cycle cut-offs without undue strain or panic effort.
6. Condensing and presenting accounting data in written or oral form to managers.
7. Using time efficiently by setting priorities, laying out and planning tasks, and following instructions and procedures.
8. Exchanging information with others inside and outside the department in a timely, tactful, and precise manner.
9. Improving the accounting system by regularly reviewing procedures and methods of formatting in an effort to find better ways of handling accounting data.

Notice that each performance factor begins with an action verb (an "ing" verb), followed by what is acted on, which is then followed by additional information about the context of the job in question. Hence, we specify in performance factor 8 that this job requires the potential to *exchange information* with certain people—*employees both in and out of the financial controls department*—and in a certain way—*in a timely, tactful, and precise manner.* In the interview you need to assess an applicant's previous experience in this activity or knowledge of how to go about it. Each performance factor is a standard against which each applicant is evaluated. The more precise and clearly defined the standard is, the easier task you will have in evaluating the applicant's potential to meet that standard successfully. Finally, notice that the performance factors are in behavioral terms. Each refers to what jobholders *do*, not what they *are*. If your organization has position descriptions, they will be helpful in identifying the performance factors to be assessed in the selection interview.

**Step 2: Write hypothetical situations.**   The information that you must probe is listed in the left-hand column of Figure 2.1. It is

1.   Previous work and nonwork experience
2.   Previous education and training
3.   Current behavior

I recommend a semistructured approach to the interview and therefore advise against entering the interview with a lengthy list of prepared questions. I do make one exception to this recommendation, however. I suggest that, in planning the interview, you write out one hypothetical situation for each of the performance factors you have identified in step 1. These hypothetical situations should be brief descriptions of a situation which a new jobholder might encounter which would require him or her to perform the factor well. An example for "exchanging information with others inside and outside the department in a timely, tactful, and precise manner" might be like the following:

> Suppose that, a day before a major closing date, you request some routine cost figures from an operations department, and they tell you they won't have the figures until next week. What steps would you take to get your figures before closing?

These hypothetical situations essentially *simulate* a part of the job that requires an applicant to show potential in a given performance factor. They would not necessarily be used with every applicant. You may use them, however, if you see no clear evidence of an applicant's potential to perform a given performance factor in either that applicant's previous work and nonwork experience or in his or her training and education. If you as an interviewer have no evidence that the applicant has ever done the performance factor or that the applicant has ever learned how to do it, your last alternative is to throw the applicant into a situation requiring it and see how he or she claims the performance would be.

*What if the interview is not for a specific job?* There are many instances in which you may not be interviewing for a specific job. This often occurs in recruiting interviews on college campuses or with applicants who just walk into the personnel office. Confronted with this situation, interviewers often move into the middle column of Figure 2.1 and do a character analysis of the applicant. There is a better option. Frequently in campus recruiting, interviewers may not be interviewing for a specific job, but they are screening for a family of jobs in a particular functional area. For example, a recruiter of marketing students might be planning to fill either a market research position or an assistant product manager's job. Similarly, in the clerical area, a recruiter may be interviewing for any one job in a progression ranging from receptionist to clerk typist to stenographer. It is often possible to group these jobs into *families* of jobs with common performance factors. In step 1, you would then identify performance factors which are necessary to the successful performance of each job in the family. You would then evaluate all applicants in terms of their potential to perform each performance factor which is common to all jobs in the family. Whether an applicant is more suitable for one job or another in the family would then depend on his or her *level* of potential to perform the performance factors.

*What if the interview is not for a family of jobs?* Some personnel specialists find themselves in the situation in which they don't know what job the applicant is applying for or they have minimal knowledge of the job to be filled. This frequently happens with first interviews in the office or on campus. This is the most difficult interview to conduct because you are essentially working in a vacuum. It is in this situation that you must resist

strongly the natural tendency to assess the applicant as a person
and hence focus on the middle column in Figure 2.1.

There is an alternative. In this situation you are not really
conducting a selection interview. Instead, you are doing a general
skills inventory on the applicant. Therefore, I recommend that
you conduct an assessment of the applicant's *potential to perform*
general performance factors that are common to a variety of jobs.
The performance factors in which the applicant shows greatest
potential will point to the appropriate job opportunities to be considered later in a more focused and tailored interview. The following performance factors are common to many jobs and will form a
good starting point for this type of assessment. They can be included in a general interview rating form like that shown in Figure
2.2.

1. Communicating
2. Utilizing time, equipment, or people
3. Applying technical knowledge and skill
4. Working with people
5. Managing employees
6. Training and developing employees
7. Controlling costs
8. Dealing with unexpected circumstances
9. Developing new ideas and methods
10. Planning and organizing

*What if the interview is to select trainees?* This is the situation in which interviewers are most prone to do a character
analysis of applicants. They are looking for potential to learn and
develop so that the applicant can move into higher-level jobs
within the organization. This look ahead to higher-level jobs is
also common among recruiters interviewing for a specific entry-
level position. A fundamental question is, "Which job are you trying to fill—the first one, the next step up, middle management ten
years from now, or what?" A rule of thumb is this: The farther
into the future you try to predict performance, the more likely
you are to be wrong. There is only so much the interview or any

## FIGURE 2.2

## Screening Interview Record

| SCHOOL | | | | | | DATE OF INTERVIEW | |
|---|---|---|---|---|---|---|---|
| PROSPECT'S NAME (LAST, FIRST, INITIAL) | | | | | | DATE AVAILABLE | |
| SCHOOL ADDRESS | | | | | | SCHOOL PHONE NO. | |
| PERMANENT ADDRESS | | | | | | PERMANENT PHONE NO. | |

| DEGREE | MAJOR | MINOR | GPA: OVERALL | MAJOR | DATE OF GRADUATION |
|---|---|---|---|---|---|
| DEGREE | MAJOR | MINOR | GPA: OVERALL | MAJOR | DATE AVAILABLE |

JOB PREFERENCE
1.   2.   3.

LOCATION PREFERENCE
1.   2.   3.

REASON FOR PREFERENCE

| | PLEASE CIRCLE YOUR EVALUATION | | | |
|---|---|---|---|---|
| EVALUATION OF CANDIDATE'S POTENTIAL TO PERFORM* | FULLY QUALIFIED | COMPETENT BUT NEEDS TRAINING | MARGINAL | UNQUALI-FIED |
| 1. Communicating | 6 5 | 4 3 | 2 1 | 0 |
| 2. Utilizing time, equipment or people | 6 5 | 4 3 | 2 1 | 0 |
| 3. Applying technical knowledge and skill | 6 5 | 4 3 | 2 1 | 0 |
| 4. Working with people | 6 5 | 4 3 | 2 1 | 0 |
| 5. Managing employees | 6 5 | 4 3 | 2 1 | 0 |
| 6. Training and developing employees | 6 5 | 4 3 | 2 1 | 0 |
| 7. Controlling costs | 6 5 | 4 3 | 2 1 | 0 |
| 8. Dealing with unexpected circumstances | 6 5 | 4 3 | 2 1 | 0 |
| 9. Developing new ideas and methods | 6 5 | 4 3 | 2 1 | 0 |
| 10. Planning and organizing | 6 5 | 4 3 | 2 1 | 0 |
| CANDIDATE'S WORK INTEREST AND MOTIVATION | PLEASE CIRCLE YOUR EVALUATION | | | |
| 1. Interest in XYZ Corporation | 6 5 | 4 3 | 2 1 | 0 |
| 2. Interest in field of work | 6 5 | 4 3 | 2 1 | 0 |
| 3. Clarity of career goals | 6 5 | 4 3 | 2 1 | 0 |
| 4. Personal suitability as co-worker | 6 5 | 4 3 | 2 1 | 0 |

ADDITIONAL COMMENTS IN SUPPORT OF THE RATINGS ABOVE

*NOTE. If interviewers are tailoring their interviews to the job, this section could be left blank. Interviewers could then write in the job's performance factors and rate applicants on that specific set of factors, rather than on the general factors included below.

other selection device can do. The changes that occur in people during the early stages of their careers have a tremendous and largely unpredictable impact on how they perform several years hence. Therefore, keep your target realistic. Consider the first and second job or the training period and the first job after training. Identify the performance factors in these two targets and then in the interview assess potential to perform these specific factors. You may develop a "gut feel" that one applicant has the personal characteristics to go far and fast, but this is highly inferential. And remember when interviewing trainees that the job of trainee can be defined and performance factors can be identified just as in any other job. It is not necessary to focus on the middle column in Figure 2.1 just because you are interviewing for a training position.

## SELECTION INTERVIEWING AND THE LAW

So far in this chapter, we have seen that we can avoid several pit-falls that undermine the reliability and validity of the selection interview by knowing our objectives, using job-related criteria for evaluating applicants, and tailoring the interview to the job. There is one final pitfall of which all selection interviewers must be aware to ensure that the content of their interviews is beyond reproach.

Since 1915 evidence has accumulated that the interview is not a very effective selection device. The continued use of invalid interviews has cost organizations significantly. Applicants who were capable of performing successfully on the job have been rejected, and applicants have been hired only to fail to perform well. Since the middle 1960s, however, poorly trained interviewers may lead to costs far greater than poor use of human resources. A myriad of legislation, executive orders, and regulations of the federal and state governments now makes every selection interviewer liable for a suit against his or her organization for discrimination against applicants on the basis of race, color, sex, national origin, handicap, veteran status, religion, or age. Let's begin by summarizing the major legislation;[8] then we will discuss how it influences the selection interviewing process.[9]

The most publicized federal law and the one most often cited by persons who feel they have been discriminated against is Title VII of the *Civil Rights Act of 1964.* This federal law prohibits discrimination in employment with respect to the terms, conditions, and privileges of employment on the basis of race, color, religion, sex, or national origin. This is the broadest of the equal employment opportunity (EEO) laws and covers such areas of employment as job assignments, training programs, discipline, and promotion.

*The Age Discrimination in Employment Act of 1967* is a federal law that prohibits discrimination against applicants and employees aged forty through seventy in terms of hiring, compensation, discharge, and other major aspects of employment. The statute requires a company to judge an applicant without any consideration of age. Although work experience is a legitimate factor to consider in any employment decision, the fact that an employee "has been around for a long time" and is between the ages of forty and seventy is prohibited by the act to be taken into account in a manner that adversely affects the employee.

*The Vocational Rehabilitation Act of 1973* makes it illegal for companies with federal contracts and subcontracts to discriminate against a physically or mentally handicapped person for reasons that have nothing to do with his or her ability to perform a job. Furthermore, Section 503 of the act requires such companies to take affirmative action to employ and advance in employment qualified handicapped individuals. This same section dictates that federal contractors make reasonable accommodation for the physical or mental limitations of an employee or an applicant for employment.

*The Vietnam-Era Veterans Readjustment Assistance Act of 1974* forbids employment discrimination against veterans of the Vietnam era and all disabled veterans. Moreover, this act goes on to require that all organizations with government contracts take affirmative action to employ and advance in employment such individuals.

## IMPLICATIONS OF EEO LEGISLATION

This legislation and succeeding court decisions have had two major effects on selection procedures. First, organizations have become increasingly more careful to use only tests which they can demonstrate do not discriminate against women or minorities. Second, more and more organizations are reducing their use of tests for selection and are relying more heavily on the interview as a selection device. They have turned to the interview under the *false* assumption that Title VII of the Civil Rights Act, as amended in 1972, applies only to tests and not to interviews. In fact, 1966 EEOC guidelines state in Section 1607.13 that interviews are selection devices and therefore must be shown not to discriminate against women or minorities. Moreover, the Uniform Guidelines on Employee Selection Procedures of 1978 restated that the guidelines of Title VII of the Civil Rights Act of 1964, as amended

by the Equal Employment Opportunity Act of 1972, ". . . apply
to tests and other selection procedures which are used as a basis
for any employment decision."

A crucial aspect of all this legislation is that, in determining
whether illegal discrimination has occurred, the courts consider
the effects on results of the practice or policy, *not the intent.* Most
interviewers do not intentionally discriminate against members of
the classes of people covered by civil rights legislation. Acting in
good faith, however, does not constitute an acceptable defense to
a charge of discrimination. Thus, questioning techniques and
subtle inferences which interviewers apply to some groups of applicants (e.g., she's married and will therefore be less likely to
transfer to another city than a married male) may be discriminating *in their effect.*

Simply stated, Title VII as well as most of the other laws prohibits two main types of employment practices and policies. The
first is the kind which treats some individuals differently in an
adverse manner on the basis of their race, color, religion, national
origin, or sex. This is called *disparate treatment.*

The second type of prohibited employer conduct is that
which generates an unjustifiable, disproportionately negative effect on any individual or group of applicants for employment who
are members of a protected class. This type of prohibited action is
said to produce an *adverse impact* which is not justified by the
employer's legitimate need to operate a safe, efficient, or pro-
fitable business.

For example, asking applicants if they have ever been arrested (not convicted) is unlawful because minorities like blacks
and Mexican-Americans are more likely in our society to be arrested than are whites. Therefore, screening out applicants on the
basis of their arrest record, rather than conviction record, is seen
as having an adverse impact on the minorities in question.

Title VII is a complaint-oriented law. That is to say, any person who feels he or she has been discriminated against may file a
complaint with the government against the employer. When a
complaint is filed, the Equal Employment Opportunity Commission, created by Title VII to enforce the law, sends a notice to the
employer and the agency initiates an investigation of the com-

plaint to discover if there does exist a sufficient basis in fact to support the allegations contained in the complaint. Title VII grants to the EEOC broad investigatory power and access to all relevant employment records and documents.

If the EEOC finds that there is reasonable cause to believe that illegal discrimination has taken place, the EEOC will so notify the company and attempt to settle the complaint through conciliation. If this attempt at settlement fails, then the EEOC or the charging party may file a lawsuit against the company. Such legal action could result in forced "quota" hiring, reinstatement, or back pay for the suing party as well as for numerous other individuals if it is a lawsuit involving a whole group of applicants.

## EFFECTS OF EEO LEGISLATION ON SELECTION INTERVIEWING

In essence, this investigatory procedure requires an employer to demonstrate its innocence. This has significant implications for what kind of information interviewers collect in the selection interview, the questions they ask, the basis for their employment decisions, and the records they keep to support their decisions.

### INFORMATION COLLECTED IN THE INTERVIEW

Extensive legislation prohibits withholding employment from applicants on the basis of race, sex, religious affiliation, national origin, color, handicapped status, or veteran status. Quite simply, these acts restrict the topics which interviewers may discuss in the interview, that is, the questions they may legally ask. Questions which appear to be entirely innocent and naïve may cost an organization a lawsuit. The rule of thumb is, *When in doubt, don't ask.* Many interviewers become annoyed with what they perceive as extreme restrictions imposed by the EEO legislation. But, remember, this legislation favors the complainant. If a topic is raised in the interview, it may influence the decision to hire or reject an applicant. The only way in which you can prove that your employment decisions did not discriminate against protected classes of applicants is not to have discussed topics that would identify the applicant as a member of that protected class.

A more positive way of viewing EEO guidelines is to ask yourself what possible relevance could these topics have to job performance? If your objective is to identify people who can do the job, EEO legislation does not restrict you from any job-related source of information. Hence, a more positive guideline is, *Ask what will help you predict the applicant's potential to perform.* Let's have a look at some potentially troublesome topics.

1. Birthplace
2. Birthplace of parents, spouse, or other close relatives
3. If applicant is a naturalized citizen
4. Foreign languages applicant reads, writes, or speaks fluently
5. How applicant acquired fluency in foreign languages
6. Wife's maiden name
7. Mother's maiden name
8. Names of brothers and sisters
9. Names of relatives other than spouse, father, or minor dependents

All these topics are questionable and should be avoided except in special instances. They all provide information about an applicant's national origin or ethnic background. If the job required fluency in a foreign language, question 4 is acceptable, but question 5 should be avoided. You might be interested in learning about all of this information as you get to know a person, *but not in the selection interview.* That's the key.

You may inquire into the applicant's right to work in the United States. This can be legally established through such inquiries as

10. If the applicant is a U.S. citizen
11. Asking to view the applicant's permanent residence visa

Consider the following:

12. If applicant has ever worked under another name
13. If applicant has child care problems
14. Marital status
15. Information regarding spouse's job plans
16. Number of children

Each of the inquiries may be interpreted as discriminating against women or married people. These topics are particularly risky if they are addressed with female applicants but not with male applicants. Some interviewers try to protect themselves by asking questions 13 and 15 of *all* applicants, male and female, but I do not recommend this practice for two reasons. First, any woman who is likely to take offense to 13 and 15 will not know that the interviewer is discussing these topics with male applicants as well. If we remember that interviewers have the objective of attracting applicants as well as assessing them, highly sensitive topics may jeopardize this objective.

A second reason for avoiding such topics is related to your view of the applicant as a responsible adult. If you explain clearly the conditions of employment and the demands of the job, most applicants will consider these factors when making their decision to accept an offer of employment. A male or female who prefers not to travel or be transferred will in most cases not accept a job requiring extensive travel.

Now let's take a look at another set of topics:

17. If applicant has ever been arrested
18. Type of discharge from military service
19. Names of clubs, societies, and lodges to which applicant belongs
20. Whether applicant owns a car
21. Whether applicant lives in a house or an apartment
22. Whether applicant owns or rents a home

Each of these topics may contribute to adverse impact on a protected class of employees. That is, screening applicants on these topics may lead to an unjustifiable negative effect on a protected group. For example, blacks and Mexican-Americans, compared with whites, are more likely to have been arrested (without necessarily having been convicted) or to have received a dishonorable discharge from military service. Employers who screen out applicants on these grounds had better be prepared to demonstrate that doing so leads to high levels of job performance. Similarly, questions 19–22 reflect socioeconomic status and may therefore be seen as having adverse impact against blacks and certain ethnic groups. These topics are best avoided in the interview.

A couple of job-related topics simply should not be addressed in the interview. They are

23. Height and weight
24. If applicant has a disability

These are topics which are properly assessed by a doctor in a physical examination. Interviewers are not qualified to assess the impact that physical factors may have on job performance. Furthermore, if the job involves hard physical labor, such as lifting over thirty pounds of weight, do not try to judge the applicant's ability to handle physical labor on the basis of his or her height and weight. Someone who is 5'3" and weighs 115 pounds may be deceptively strong. In addition, these height and weight requirements may have an adverse impact on women and some ethnic groups who are generally smaller in stature then are many males. Leave assessments of the applicant's ability to perform physical labor to proper medical personnel.

Finally, interviewers may not legally ask the applicant's age, because employers are prohibited from discriminating against applicants between forty and seventy years of age. Interviewers may ask, however, for verification that the applicant is over eighteen years of age as this is the minimum age for many types of jobs.

## WHAT CAN BE ASKED?

The subject of EEO guidelines and restrictions is often rather exasperating to interviewers because the emphasis is quite negative. After hearing all the topics they cannot discuss, some interviewers feel like throwing up their hands and asking, "What's left for me to talk about?" The answer is brief but truly offers a great deal of fruitful territory. Interviewers should focus on

1. What the applicant has done in the past—this includes previous work experience and also nonwork experience such as extracurricular activities, hobbies, and interests in which the applicant may have performed functions which could be used on the job.
2. What the applicant has learned in the past—this includes formal education and course work as well as training courses in which the applicant may have learned something which could be applied on the job.

A semistructured interview that has been tailored to the job and based on genuine job requirements will focus on the two points just listed. If you follow the approach recommended in this chapter, you should have no EEO problems.

## BASIS FOR THE EVALUATION

The most significant influence of EEO legislation on the selection process concerns the basis on which the selection decision is made. The acts cited earlier state explicitly that people cannot be denied employment on the basis of specific factors.

In the selection interview, this legislation relates directly to the basis on which the applicant is evaluated. The interview is the most highly subjective of the available selection devices and is therefore most open to claims of discrimination. Even careful avoidance of the topics itemized in the last section may not be an adequate defense. This is because age, sex, physical handicap, race, and ethnic background may be ascertained through observation or attention to surnames. How, then, can the interviewer ensure a defense against charges of unlawful discrimination?

The best defense is a sound alternative. That is, if you as an interviewer can explain and point to the basis of your preferences for one applicant over another, you are in a strong position. One of the greatest tragedies in interviewing is how much information gathered in the interview is thrown away in the evaluation process. A distressingly large percentage of interviewers reduce a half hour or more of sound, job-related discussion into a "gut feel" expressed in a few words ("he impressed me") or a series of ratings of highly subjective traits like those seen in the middle column of Figure 2.1. Throwing away so much information in the evaluation process is not only inefficient, but it is also highly risky. What's to prevent a rejected applicant from pointing to an interviewer and charging discrimination?

The alternative is to rate the applicant in terms of potential to perform specific job functions. This is the evaluation process discussed in relation to Figure 2.1. Having recorded evaluations of the applicant's potential to perform factors like those in the right-hand column of Figure 2.1, and having notes to support these ratings, is the best defense against claims of discrimination. The more job-related and specific the evaluation, the better the defense.

## DATA RETENTION

The third influence of EEO legislation on selection procedures concerns the retention of information on which the selection decision was made. The Uniform Guidelines of 1978 require that employers "should maintain and have available for inspection records or other information which will disclose the impact which its tests and other selection procedures have upon employment opportunities of persons by identifiable race, sex, or ethnic group" (Section 4A). Many interviewers record little or nothing after the interview. Others simply jot a few notes on an application form or resumé and toss it into a file. I recommend that evaluations of potential to perform and supportive notes be recorded for every applicant and that these records be retained for at least six months. The nature of these evaluations is discussed later in this chapter. Then if challenged to produce proof of nondiscrimination, the employer has good information to fall back on.

## CONDUCTING THE SELECTION INTERVIEW

Conducting interviews is truly an art. Planning them and setting out their content can be learned by following the guidelines already noted, but the result is merely the skeleton of the interview. Adding flesh to the skeleton and bringing the interview to life is a subtle and highly developed skill. This section presents guidance for conducting selection interviews and illustrates this art by example.

### PREPARATION FOR THE INTERVIEW

Let's just briefly review the steps to be taken to prepare the content of the interview. The interviewer and the applicant both have objectives of information giving, information receiving, and testing personal chemistry. Therefore I have suggested a six-point format that meets all these objectives. The job to be filled must be analyzed so that the performance factors that make up the job can be listed. This preparation leads to a semistructured interview that is tailored to a specific job. Hypothetical situations have been written to test the applicant's potential to perform the factors. Awareness of EEO guidelines ensures that a lawful interview will be conducted. Finally, an application form or resumé usually provides a preview of the applicant and can be examined before the interview. The next step is simply to take all this preparation and convert it into a smooth, relaxed, conversational interview. Let's see how we do this.

**The application or resumé.** A cardinal rule of selection interviewing is to review the application or resumé *before* beginning the interview. If you find yourself in a situation in which interviewees arrive with resumé in hand, ask them to wait for a couple of minutes while you review it.

We review the application or resumé for several reasons. First, we check for any clear discrepancy between the paper qualifications of the applicant and the job specifications. By job specifications I mean the minimal qualifications required of all applicants (e.g., degrees, areas of specialization, related work experience). If on paper the applicant seems to be an obvious mismatch for the job, no interview is necessary unless you wish to assess the applicant's general potential and then look for a suitable job in your organization.

Assuming that the applicant has the minimal paper qualifications, the review then turns toward information that needs to be probed for signs of the applicant's intention and potential to do the job. Let's consider intention first.

> Is the applicant currently employed?
>
> If so, why is the interviewee leaving his or her current job?
>
> Why is the applicant interested in your organization?
>
> Is a career change involved? Why the change?
>
> Is the interviewee applying for a similar job or one that is a step up in a career progression?
>
> If the applicant is a student, what interest does he or she have in the career your organization offers?

These are just a few questions that you will need to pursue with an applicant, depending on his or her current situation. As you review the resumé or application, look for points that raise questions about the applicant's intention to perform for your organization.

Now let's consider the applicant's *potential* to perform the job. Look first at previous work experience which may have involved some of the performance factors that make up the job you are filling. When interviewing students who have no related work experience, look for extracurricular activities or hobbies which may have involved some of your performance factors. Did the president of the marketing club plan, organize, schedule, or lead others? Did the applicant with extensive part-time work experience have success in planning and organizing time and dealing with stress? With students, look for courses related to your job which would have taught potential to perform. Especially fertile territory is a project in which the student was required to apply material learned in the courses. In reviewing previous work and nonwork experience, education, and training, you are looking for signs of potential to perform the factors you must assess in the interview.

Finally, in reviewing the resumé or application form, you need to look for a rapport builder—something you have in common with the applicant. Look for a common hobby, interest, school, or area of the country which you can use to break the ice at the beginning of the interview.

In summary, then, review the applicant on paper with the following goals in mind:

1.  Check the basic paper qualifications for the job.
2.  Find a rapport builder.
3.  Look for signs of intention to pursue a given career and signs of interest in your organization.
4.  Look for signs of past experiences or education which can be probed to assess potential to perform your job's performance factors.

**Information you will provide the applicant.**   A major objective of the selection interview is to provide information about the job and organization. How well this is done will strongly affect your organization's image and attractiveness to the applicant. Furthermore, during that interview you are the personification of your organization, and how you conduct yourself will influence the applicant far more significantly than all the brochures, annual reports, and organizational charts you can muster. In short, you need to be a professional and appear to have done your homework.

More specifically, recruiters must be armed with information that prospective employees will find useful. In particular it is very helpful for company recruiters who visit university campuses to get together and decide what information is best covered in recruiting brochures and literature and what topics need attention in the actual interview. Generally, students as well as applicants with more work experience want to learn details of the job for which they are applying. They want to know what a typical day on the job is like and the kind of people they will be working with. They are also very interested in the organization's opportunities for training and career development. Above all, they want to be told the truth; a hard sell will not only turn off applicants, but it will also increase turnover due to high expectations which are not met.[10]

## DURING THE INTERVIEW

Even though you have a six-point format and a list of performance factors and hypothetical situations, your aim is for the interview to appear unplanned and unstructured. The result is a conversational interview in which applicants feel relaxed and in which they feel that you were genuinely interested in them because you talked so much about topics they raised that were important to them. *The key to a conversational selection interview is to get the applicant to raise many of the topics you want to discuss and then to focus on them.* You can reach this goal by following the sequence described in Chapter 1. These steps, when applied to the selection interview, are

> Initiate
>
> Listen
>
> Focus
>
> Probe
>
> Evaluate

Let's consider each of these steps and the techniques which they involve.

**Initiate.**    First, I want to refresh your memory of the overall format of the selection interview. The six steps are as follows:

1. Build rapport
2. Set the agenda
3. Gather information
   a. Intention to perform the job
   b. Potential to perform the job

4.   Provide information about the job and organization
5.   Answer questions
6.   Terminate

You will begin by talking about something you have in common with the applicant for about a minute and then setting the agenda. At this point you must begin the body of the interview. You need to gather information on the applicant's intention and potential to do the job. A good rule of thumb is to *begin on the applicant's home territory*. With an experienced applicant, initiate the discussion with a question about the most recent job. You want the applicant to raise your performance factors. Open-ended questions are useful here. For example,

**Initiate**

"I see that you are currently employed as an administrative assistant. Basically what does that job consist of?"

or

"Would you please summarize your major responsibilities in your job as an administrative assistant?"

With students who have no related work experience, you must begin with extracurricular activities or training and education. Examples are

**Initiate**

"I see that you were president of the marketing club. What did that entail?"

or

"I notice that your major in business school is accounting. How did you happen to choose that field?"

or

"What kind of work do you hope to do with your marketing background?"

Your intention is to get applicants talking about specific job functions which they are currently performing or would like to perform.

**Listen.**    At this point you must simply listen very carefully for topics you wish to pursue. In particular you are listening for some of the performance factors on your list. Careful preparation really pays off here. It stills that little voice in many interviewers' minds which sometimes cries out, "What am I going to say when the applicant stops talking?"

It is important to respond nonverbally to applicants when they are talking. Applicants like to know that the interviewer is alive and well and are sometimes not really sure when they are confronted with a blank face staring back at them. A simple head nod or "um huh" and a lean forward in a chair shows interest and encourages the applicant to continue talking.

**Focus and probe.**    Interviewers do their real work in these two steps. There are a variety of techniques, listed now, that will help you focus and probe. *Remember that overindulgence in any of these techniques is bad.* But each one helps focus the discussion and stimulates the applicant to say more. Let's review them quickly:

1. *Head nod; um huh.* This simple response lets applicants know you are listening and stimulates them to say more.

2. *Reflecting ideas.* Here you simply paraphrase what the applicant has just said. This is particularly useful to focus the discussion on a particular part of the applicant's response. For example,

INTERVIEWER:   "I notice that you were president of the marketing club. What did that involve?"

APPLICANT:   "Well, there were a variety of things involved. I organized an advisory group of five people employed with large marketing firms. I was also responsible for scheduling and advertising our biweekly meetings, and I actually ran the meetings as well."

INTERVIEWER:   "So you put together this advisory group."

APPLICANT:   "Oh, yes. Now that was a new idea I thought would make it easier for us to find guest speakers, and so I . . ."

Notice that, in reflecting one point of the three raised by the applicant, the interviewer was able to focus on that particular topic.

3. *Reflecting feelings.* Making contact with someone on a feeling level gives the interview a personal touch that will make a lasting impression on the applicant. This is particularly useful when you detect excitement or strong interest on the part of the applicant. Saying, "You really sound excited about that part of your work" is a good example. Reflecting feelings is also a good way to examine intention and interest. If you detect a low level of interest and enthusiasm as the applicant discusses a topic, you might say,

INTERVIEWER:   "You know, I get the feeling that accounting wasn't your favorite course."
APPLICANT:   "Well, I must admit I wasn't too fond of the highly numbers-oriented courses. I much prefer working with people."

4. *Summarizing.* This is particularly useful for making smooth transitions, as noted in Chapter 1. The key to a conversational interview is to make sure every question fits easily into the flow of the interview. When you need to change topics, therefore, it is useful to summarize the topics you are leaving, say that you'd like to turn to something else, and then ask the next question (see the example in Chapter 1).

5. *Question.* Questions may be open ended or quite focused. Open-ended questions open a topic up for discussion. Consider the following examples:

"What was your involvement in . . .?"
"What were your major responsibilities as . . .?"
"How did you handle a situation like . . .?"
"In that job, how did you apply . . .?"
"What did you learn that you feel would help you perform . . .?"

The specific probe is more focused and is best used with a transitional statement, such as in the following examples:

> "You mentioned that working with this kind of employee was challenging. In what way?"
>
> "I'm particularly interested in your comment about motivating people. What have you learned in your course work to help you motivate people?"
>
> "That's a very interesting conclusion you just made about. . . . How did you happen to come to that conclusion?"

These transitional statements are very useful to encourage your applicant to focus on the question and to say more.

As noted earlier, overindulgence in any of these techniques is bad. Many interviewers rely too heavily on the question, and this can cause the interview to take on the question–answer, question–answer, question–answer flavor of an interrogation. This type of interview does little to attract the applicant to you and your organization. On the other hand, heavy reliance on nondirective techniques can be very annoying. Wagging your head for twenty minutes and muttering "um huh" won't do you much good, and extensive reflecting may make the applicant wonder if there is an echo in the interview room. The art of interviewing is in using the appropriate technique at the right time to meet your objectives.

## ADDITIONAL REMINDERS

**Eye contact, body language, and voice.** Have you every noticed how seldom people actually look at one another when they are speaking? Many of us look off somewhere, and, then, when we finish our question or answer, we swing our eyes back to the other person. Interviewers, look your applicants in the eye when you are talking with them! Now this can be overdone, of course, but direct eye contact and using the applicant's name makes the interview more personal.

And be aware of your body position and voice. One of the

worst enemies of the interviewer is fatigue or lack of interest, both of which show up in posture and voice. A monotone delivery of information about the job and company can be deadly. As a representative of your organization in the interview, you are performing and you must work hard to keep your energy level high. If you are interested in what the applicant has just said, allow yourself to lean forward and let the pitch and volume of your voice rise. If you are bored, struggle not to show it. Picture yourself in the middle of the afternoon, slouched in your chair, looking into space, and saying in a weak monotone, "I'm really interested in your application; you have a very strong set of qualifications." This just won't work. What you say means less than how you say it.

**Leading questions, multiple questions, or supplying the answer.** It is surprising to realize how much of our own opinions or ideas we communicate in the way we phrase our questions. Consider the following examples:

"Don't you think you are better suited for clerical work?"

"Wouldn't you find it difficult adapting to big city life?"

"You have had supervisory experience, haven't you?"

These are called leading questions because they suggest an answer. In the first example, the interviewer is asking the applicant to agree with the opinion that he or she is applying for the wrong job. Some of us even ask and answer our own questions, giving the applicant the opportunity to lean back, relax, and think, "keep it up, you're doing great." For example, an interviewer may say, "How did you become interested in banking? You mentioned earlier that your father was a banker; that was probably a major influence." For a good illustration of this questioning technique, just tune in any TV talk show and listen carefully to how the host directs the conversation by asking leading questions or answering his or her own questions.

Another common fault is for the interviewer to ask a number of questions in a series before allowing the applicant a chance to respond. For example,

INTERVIEWER:    "When confronted with a problem, what approach do you
take to problem solving? Do you like a structured approach or one in
which you use your creativity in a less systematic way? How successful
have you been?"

APPLICANT:    "I feel I've been very successful in solving the problems I've
faced."

Here the interviewer should have stopped with the first question.
The second question leads the applicant by providing two alternatives, and the third question is related to the first two, but is different. Notice that the applicant answered the last question, which
is quite common. The general rule is to ask the first question and
then sit back and listen. Then probe the applicant's response for
more detail.

## GUIDE FOR GATHERING INFORMATION

We have discussed how interviewers can initiate, listen, focus,
and probe to learn whether applicants will and can perform the
job. Before we deal with the last step—evaluate—we need to consider how the information can be collected and used as efficiently
as possible. We know that work and nonwork experience, training, and education are the territories we need to probe into with
the applicant. It is in these areas that interviewers discover the
performance factors that the applicant has either done before or
learned how to do in the past. How interviewers collect this information is a crucial issue in conducting the interview. Now here I
am referring to phase 3 in the overall format for the selection interview: gather information.

**Resumé as a guide.**    Most interviewers use the resumé or application form as a guide for gathering information. They review
the resumé or application form, working through it section by section, and probe into work experience, education, extracurricular
activities, and so on. Then, after the interview is over, they
scratch their heads and try to recall what the applicant said about
each of their performance factors.

This procedure is relatively unfocused and inefficient. There is an easier way. Let's review what we know about human interviewers. We know that they forget, form first impressions and jump to conclusions, make unsupported inferences, and selectively distort or ignore information. If interviewers follow the resumé as a guide and review all the applicant's previous work and nonwork experience, training, and education, these processes can and do still operate. Interviewers forget. They form a favorable first impression and therefore minimize the applicant's lack of experience in, for example, budgeting. They forget to ask specifically about the applicant's method of supervision in a previous job. After the interview is over and they are rating the applicant, they may find themselves hampered because they have forgotten or distorted some information and have neglected to cover other relevant topics. How often have you felt exasperated after an interview because you forgot to ask the applicant something important?

**Performance factors as a guide.**  In examining an applicant's potential to perform the job, we need a format that forces the interviewer to probe systematically into all relevant topics in spite of human frailties. That format is based on the performance factors that make up the job. Rather than reviewing the resumé globally, interviewers need to cover the past in a more focused way. If seven performance factors have been identified for the job, they need to probe into the applicant's past seven times, each time focusing on one of the seven performance factors. Although interviewers might think this procedure would appear repetitive or stilted, it can be done after a little practice as a smooth conversation with no apparent structure. Here's how to do it.

The best predictor of future performance is past performance. Hence, interviewers need to begin by determining whether the applicant has ever done any of the performance factors in the past. The place to start is previous work or nonwork experience. Begin by initiating the discussion with an open-ended question about the applicant's previous job or an extracurricular activity or a course that involved project work. The previous section contained several examples of questions to initiate the discussion. The intention is to get the applicant talking about something he or she *has done.*

Then listen very carefully for some of your performance factors and store them in your mind. Focus on one of them. Let's say, for example, that you focus on the supervisory responsibility of the previous job or the extent to which the student directed the work of other students in the role as president of the marketing club. You then proceed to ask the applicant questions about how he or she supervised, why, with what results, and so on. You may want to ask about any training the applicant has had in supervisory skills and how he or she would apply it to your situation. Here is where the previously prepared hypothetical example may be used. You can simply ask an applicant how he or she might handle the situation which you describe. After you have questioned the applicant until you feel you know his or her potential to supervise on the job, you rate the applicant at that point by jotting down a number from 1 to 10, where 1 represents the lowest potential to supervise successfully. I suggest that you rate, first, during the interview when the information is freshest and, second, in terms of a prediction of on-the-job performance.

You then turn to another performance factor which the applicant raised in response to your initial open-ended question. Suppose that the applicant mentioned that he or she was responsible for budgeting and that budgeting is one of your performance factors. Focus on it by saying, "You mentioned earlier that you were involved in budgeting. How did you handle that function?" You repeat the focus–probe–evaluate sequence until you have covered all seven of your performance factors. In some factors the applicant may have hands-on experience and in others only training. With each factor you find out whether the applicant has ever done it before or whether the applicant has learned how to do it. You then judge how well the applicant can do it for you. The result of such an interview is a profile of ratings of the applicant's potential to perform the performance factors of the job in question (see Figure 2.3). You then turn to questions of interest and career plans to judge intention—whether the applicant *will* do the job.

When interviewers follow this approach, they systematically cover job-related topics in spite of their human biases like first impressions, jumping to conclusions, and so on. The interview is

FIGURE 2.3
Profile of Ratings

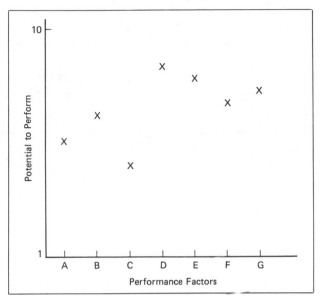

also conversational because interviewers follow up on topics raised by the applicant (which happen to be on their list of performance factors).

An added advantage of this approach is that the questions are directed toward performance. Topics prohibited by EEO legislation are much less likely to arise in a performance-based interview. The resulting profile of potential to perform, shown in Figure 2.3, is job related, and therefore can be more clearly defended as a basis of selection than ratings of ambiguous traits. Furthermore, this type of assessment is much easier for personnel specialists to communicate to supervisors and line managers for whom they may be doing initial screening. To those personnel specialists I recommend that you meet with the person who supervises the job to be filled and together work out the performance factors. The resultant performance factors can then be used by both personnel specialists and line managers as a common set of standards against which to evaluate all applicants. Having a common set of clearly defined evaluation standards will do much to improve the reliability of the selection interview.

# THE BOTTOM LINE

Now that I have covered extensively how you can plan the content of selection interviews and conduct them effectively, one question remains: "Will it work?" The bottom line on the selection interview is whether it is reliable and valid. It is up to you to examine your interviews to assess their reliability and validity.

**Reliability.** Assessing reliability is straightforward if you have designed the interview carefully and have identified the performance factors on which applicants are to be evaluated. Let's say that over the course of six months you interview fifty applicants who are subsequently seen by one or more other members of your organization. Compare your evaluations of each applicant, factor by factor, with the evaluations made by other interviewers. Check to see if the ratings are similar, differing by only a point or two on a ten-point scale. The more consistent the ratings, the more reliable the interview. It is possible to compute correlation coefficients to place a numerical value on the estimate of reliability. Anyone who interviews applicants that are also interviewed by someone else can assess reliability.

**Validity.** The first step to validity is reliability. That is, a selection device that is not reliable cannot predict performance accurately. But, if you have evidence of reliability, your next step is to determine whether your assessments of applicants' potential to perform are related to their actual performance as new employees.

Assessing validity is not nearly as straightforward as testing reliability.[11] I strongly recommend, however, that anyone who conducts selection interviews regularly perform a crude test of validity. To do so, you need to retain your evaluations of applicants (this is advisable for EEO purposes anyway), and you need to collect some measure of performance of the applicants who were hired. Here is the first practical problem in assessing validity. While you can measure the performance of those applicants you hire, you will never know how well those you rejected would have performed. You are therefore working with limited information. Let's proceed, though, and see what you can learn even from limited information.

## FIGURE 2.4
### Validating the Selection Interview

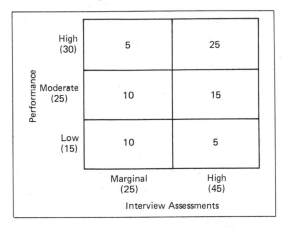

Let's consider a situation in which seventy applicants were interviewed and hired. After they have been employed for at least three months, collect their performance appraisal forms and group them into three categories of performance: high, moderate, and low.[12] (Access to performance appraisals is relatively simple if you work in the personnel department where this information is filed.) In our example in Figure 2.4, thirty are performing in the high category, twenty-five are in the moderate category, and fifteen are low. Next consult your interview records and summarize your assessments of each applicant's potential to perform as either high or marginal. In our example, forty-five fell into the high category and twenty-five were in the marginal category. Now you simply assign employees to the areas of the figure according to the categories into which they fall. Of the twenty-five marginal applicants, ten are currently low performers, ten are moderate, and only five are high. Of the forty-five applicants rated high, twenty-five are performing well, fifteen moderately, and only five are low. This crude test demonstrates a very good level of validity. More sophisticated correlational analysis of validity is also possible with relatively large numbers of applicants.

It is important that organizations examine the validity of the interview, along with all other selection devices. Only then can you interview applicants and know not only how effective you are but also how strong your evidence is against any claims of discrimination.

# 3

# *Performance Appraisal Interviewing*

"What a disappointment that was! I went into my supervisor's office expecting a pat on the back and all I got was criticism."

"These rating forms are impossible. Why do I have to do a personality analysis of my employees at appraisal time?"

"Man, was that frustrating. I wanted to talk about goal setting and all Jackson wanted to hear was how large the salary increase would be next year."

"I had such high hopes for that interview, but it was so awkward and unnatural that we never did get into a fruitful discussion."

The performance appraisal interview probably requires more skill from the interviewer than does any other interview covered in this book. Managers who have a good day-to-day relationship with their employees often see that relationship severely strained during that annual, formal interview which may be awkward and even painful to both parties. Whether on the giving or receiving end of these interviews, many employed people report extreme reactions to them. A poorly handled performance appraisal interview can depress a boss, crush an employee's morale, and send that employee directly to the help wanted or career section of the newspaper. On the other hand, an effective performance appraisal interview can be a very exhilarating and motivating experience for the boss and the employee. Unfortunately, difficulties in performance appraisal interviews have become so common that personnel specialists in organizations with formal performance appraisal systems report extreme difficulty in getting supervisors and managers even to conduct their interviews.

The performance appraisal interview is a discussion between an employee and his or her immediate supervisor that focuses on that employee's performance over the last several months and also includes some planning for changes in future performance. Organizations may refer to this type of interview with a variety of terms, such as performance review, work planning and review, performance audit, or performance evaluation, all of which have basically the same meaning. This interview differs from the day-to-day feedback and planning occurring between a boss and an employee in that it takes a longer look into the past and a longer look into the future. Performance appraisal interviews occur annually in most organizations and as often as quarterly in some.

These interviews certainly affect all of us significantly—in our pocketbooks and in the pride we take in our accomplishments at work. If we feel that we have been dealt with unfairly or insensitively in either of these areas, we are likely to feel very dissatisfied. This places added pressure on managers and supervisors to conduct skillful performance appraisal interviews. It is very unfortunate, however, that so few receive any training in how to conduct these interviews. This is not a skill that many bosses can afford to pick up by trial and error. The trials are very trying, and the errors are exceedingly costly.

## OBJECTIVES

Let's begin at the beginning. As with all the interviews in this book, the performance appraisal interview has several objectives which must be noted and carefully addressed if the interview is to succeed. They are

1. To communicate and support administrative decisions such as salary increases, promotions, and transfers.
2. To provide performance feedback to employees—tell them where they stand.
3. To promote the development of employees through identifying training needs and counseling, coaching, and motivating employees to improve.
4. To establish mutual works goals.
5. To promote career development by discussing long-range plans for development and promotion.

These objectives fall into two general categories: salary administration and employee development. Let's discuss each of these in turn.

**Salary administration.**   The first objective is the one that is often uppermost in every employee's mind at performance appraisal time—"How much more will I be paid next year?" The performance appraisal interview serves the organization's program of salary administration by providing a vehicle through which you, as an immediate supervisor, pass along decisions based on employee job performance (e.g., salary increases, promotions, and transfers) to your employees. Since a supervisor's recommendations usually strongly affect these decisions, you may be called upon in the interview to justify or even defend decisions regarding salary increases, promotions, and transfers.

**Employee development.**   The remaining four objectives fall clearly into the category of employee development. Each serves a supervisor's purpose of letting his or her employees know where they stand and helping them to improve their performance in the future.

As a supervisor, you evaluate your employees' performance and give them feedback during the interview. Feedback takes many different forms. For example, in some organizations a supervisor and an employee may discuss the employee's strengths and weaknesses informally in the interview. In other organizations, they review goals set during the last performance appraisal interview and base evaluations on how well the goals were met. In still other companies, supervisors fill out a rating form which is the basis for the feedback given to employees.

To meet the third objective, you and your employees must identify the causes of their performance. Do they need additional training to increase their skill and knowledge required to do the job? Were there factors outside their control that prevented them from reaching their goals? Here you are learning as much as possible from your employees and then coaching and motivating them so they will perform better in the future.

In the performance appraisal interview, a discussion of future plans addresses objectives 4 and 5. You and your employees may set some goals to be met during the next year. You may also discuss longer-range plans to help employees chart their careers over a number of years.

## IMPROVING THE PERFORMANCE APPRAISAL INTERVIEW

As I have already mentioned, conducting performance appraisal interviews may be the most difficult assignment which you are asked to carry out by the personnel department.[1] There are three basic reasons for this difficulty, summarized in Table 3.1. First, you have *several objectives* to meet in the performance appraisal interview, and you will have to plan it carefully to meet those objectives.

Second, every objective in the interview depends on the *measures and procedures used to appraise employee performance.* You enter the interview with an appraisal in your head or on paper. It is the basis for your salary and promotional recommendations. Your feedback to the employee draws heavily from your formal or informal appraisal. And any plans that you and your employee make for the future will be based on your appraisal of that employee. In many cases, however, the method a supervisor uses to appraise performance *before entering the interview* is highly subjective and open to challenge by the employee. If the

### TABLE 3.1
### Weaknesses of the Performance Appraisal Interview

```
  I. Multiple Objectives
     A. Conflict between salary administration and employee
        development
     B. Objectives require the interviewer to assume multiple roles
     C. Not all objectives apply to all employees

 II. Methods Used to Appraise Employee Performance
     A. Many appraisal methods are highly subjective
     B. Appraisal methods may violate EEO standards
     C. Feedback is not useful to the employee

III. Approach to the Interview
     A. Supervisors do not have a well-considered approach
     B. Different approaches work with different employees
```

appraisal method is flawed, chances are very high that you will have trouble meeting all your objectives in the interview.

Third, *how you approach the performance appraisal interview* is crucial. The appropriate approach is seldom intuitively obvious, and the skills in conducting a successful interview with a given approach are very difficult to learn by trial and error. You need to develop these skills carefully in order to conduct performance appraisal interviews successfully. Let's have a closer look at these three reasons for failure in the performance appraisal interview and see what you can do to minimize or avoid them. Steps you can take to improve your performance appraisal interviews are listed in Table 3.2.

**Multiple objectives.** As in all interviews, you have much to achieve in the performance appraisal interview. The five objectives will require you to assume two quite different roles during the interview. In one role you are primarily *giving information* to your employees. You have to do a good deal of talking and telling as you communicate your salary decisions and give them feedback on their performance. As you discuss the causes of employee performance, set mutual work goals, and discuss career plans, you assume a more passive role of *seeking information* and listening. These two roles of acting as an authority figure who delivers information but also as a consultant who listens and counsels are

## TABLE 3.2
### Improving the Performance Appraisal Interview

I. Planning the Interview to Meet Specific Objectives
A. Split salary administration and employee development into two interviews
B. Plan an interview format to meet specific objectives
C. Tailor interview objectives to the employee

II. Methods Used to Appraise Employee Performance
A. Evaluate performance and results, not personal characteristics
B. Make your appraisal method meet EEO standards
C. Make feedback useful to employees

III. Approach to the Interview
A. Plan an approach that meets your objectives
B. Tailor your approach to your employee and your own supervisory style

quite different from one another and require a good deal of skill from the interviewer.

Furthermore, there is some inherent conflict within the set of five objectives. The objective dealing with salary administration tends to take precedence over the four objectives concerning employee development.[2] In many cases as soon as the discussion turns to the percentage of salary increase or the denial of a desired promotion, goal setting and upward communication are lost in the shuffle. If the employee is unhappy with the raise, he or she may ask you to justify the decision. At this point you may present the appraisal in defense of the administrative decision, and the employee may counterattack. The discussion can degenerate into a rather heated debate in which little actual listening occurs but instead each party becomes intent on scoring points. This atmosphere is hardly conducive to a positive discussion of employee development.

**Planning the interview to meet specific objectives.** This conflict in objectives has prompted the recommendation that the two general categories of objectives—salary administration and employee development—be addressed in two separate interviews.[3] I support this recommendation. I propose that *performance appraisal interviews* be conducted in an organization approximately three months *before* salary budgets are set for the up-coming year. These performance appraisals are aimed solely at the objectives concerning employee development. When each department receives its final salary budget and salary increases are determined, then a second set of interviews can be conducted. These *salary review interviews* serve the purpose of communicating and justifying administrative decisions based on employee performance. This system of conducting the performance appraisal interview before budgets are set not only splits the difficult discussion of salary from the performance appraisal interview, but it also prevents supervisors from working backward (i.e., deciding on a merit increase and then appraising employee performance to justify the increase). Many firms are adopting the practice of conducting two separate interviews—one for performance appraisal and one for salary review. *Since this practice is becoming common, I have focused the remainder of this chapter on the performance appraisal interview dealing only with employee development.*

One more point on objectives. Before you conduct a performance appraisal interview, you should review the four objectives under employee development to determine which are appropriate for a given employee. For new, career-oriented employees all four objectives may apply. They are eager for feedback, but they are also very interested in your suggestions on how they can improve by pursuing opportunities for training and development. But not every employee is on the "fast track" to promotion. What about the reliable, above-average performers who have risen to their level in the organization and are going no farther? With these employees, you may wish to scale down the interview to giving feedback and setting goals for the next year. It is important that you have a clear plan for which objectives are most suitable for each employee you interview.

**Measures of employee performance.**    Your success or failure in the interview certainly depends heavily on how you evaluate employee performance. All four of the objectives contributing to employee development build on your organization's appraisal of employee performance. In my opinion poor methods and pro-

**TABLE 3.3**
**Performance Appraisal Methods**

| | I<br>Traits<br>(What employee is) | II<br>Performance<br>(What employee does) | III<br>Goals<br>(What employee achieves) |
|---|---|---|---|
| Information collected | | | |
| Appraisal method | 1. Trait-rating scales<br><br>2. Narrative assessments of employee worth | 1. Essay appraisals<br><br>2. Behavioral checklists<br><br>3. Behaviorally based rating scales | 1. Management by objectives<br><br>2. Work planning and review |

cedures for appraising performance are the most prevalent cause of failure in performance appraisal interviews.

Condensing an employee's performance over a period of six months or one year into a relatively concise and meaningful appraisal is difficult. The tools you have to work with strongly influence the accuracy and quality of your appraisals. Unfortunately, the appraisal tools of most organizations simply aren't very good. Most are highly subjective, whether they're a set of rating scales, or judgments about how well an employee met a goal. Of course, there is no way to eliminate the subjectivity from performance appraisal, but some procedures are better than others. Let's have a look at some common appraisal methods. I have divided them into three categories,[4] shown in Table 3.3.

**Evaluating personal traits.** Most appraisal methods evaluate *people* rather than what people do or achieve. The rating scale is the most common tool used for the subjective evaluation of employee performance. Rating scales come in many sizes and shapes, but they typically are headed by the characteristic being rated (e.g., initiative, maturity, personality). Along the continuum of the scale are numbers and usually phrases to identify different levels of the characteristic under scrutiny (e.g., excellent, average, consistently exceeds requirements). An example of a typical rating scale is given in Table 3.4.

Major problems occur when rating scales are used to evaluate employees' personal characteristics or traits. Quite simply, *the employee and the supervisor do not know what they're talking about* when they discuss ratings of traits in a performance

### TABLE 3.4
### Typical Rating Scale

| INITIATIVE |
| --- |
| 5  Exceptional |
| 4  Better than average |
| 3  Usually meets the situation |
| 2  Easily discouraged by obstacles |
| 1  Poor |

appraisal interview. Consider the case in which the supervisor has rated an employee on initiative, using the rating scale in Table 3.4.

SUPERVISOR:   "And on initiative I rated you at the '3' level which is average. I feel that you have room for improvement in this area."

EMPLOYEE:   "What do you mean by initiative?"

SUPERVISOR:   "Well, you know what initiative is; it's a kind of get-up-and-go, take-charge attitude toward your work."

EMPLOYEE:   "You mean I'm not motivated?"

SUPERVISOR:   "Well no, not exactly. You're motivated, but initiative goes beyond that. You need to be a self-starter."

EMPLOYEE:   "What's a self-starter?"

SUPERVISOR:   "Well . . ."

Have you ever been on the giving or receiving end of such a conversation? It can make you feel pretty confused. Does your organization have rating scales that require you to make judgments about the basic character of an employee? These rating scales thrust you directly into the role of judge of the employee's character. The employee becomes confused or defensive and the interview degenerates.

In some organizations, appraisals are done more informally. The supervisor may consider an employee's performance over the past year and then write out the employee's strong and weak points in narrative. Unfortunately, these narratives are often written in terms of basic personal characteristics and, therefore, suffer from the same problems of trait rating scales.

The major weakness of appraisal methods that evaluate traits is that they provide employees with feedback about what they *are* rather than what they *do*. They force the supervisor to assess unobservable, poorly defined, inferred characteristics. Supervisors do not see initiative or maturity or personality, but instead they see a large number of individual behaviors from which they have to *infer* these traits. Of course, if you and I define the trait differently, depending on our own personal experience, and if you fill out a rating scale on me, we will differ in our views of whether the ratings truly reflect how well I have performed. That leads to real trouble in the interview.

**Performance appraisal and EEO.** It is my view that evaluations of personal traits, regardless of the method used, are totally inappropriate in performance appraisal. These methods make supervisors and managers "play God" and judge employees in vague abstractions. These evaluations result in poor communication and defensiveness in the performance appraisal interview. Furthermore, highly subjective appraisal methods open organizations up to charges of discrimination against protected groups of employees.

As you may know, Title VII of the Civil Rights Act of 1964 and the Uniform Guidelines for Employee Selection of 1978 apply not only to selection but also to salary and promotion decisions concerning current employees. A good illustration of this is the case of *Rowe* v. *General Motors Corporation,* in which the Court of Appeals for the Fifth Circuit ruled that blacks had been unfairly denied promotions and transfers because the performance appraisal on which the promotions and transfers were based were subjective and vague.[5] In short, a supervisor can be charged with unlawful discrimination by an employee of a protected class who feels he or she was denied a raise or promotion on the basis of factors unrelated to performance. Appraisal methods that evaluate employee traits are wide open to charges of discrimination. If an organization's managers and supervisors are evaluating employees on the basis of highly subjective ratings of personal characteristics, an employee can argue that a personal bias exists toward him or her. What's to prevent a woman from charging that a male supervisor rated her low on maturity because she is a woman? What's to prevent a black employee from claiming that a low rating on motivation was based on a stereotype about blacks? How can any organization justify ratings of personal traits?

## *APPRAISING PERFORMANCE OR RESULTS*

How can an organization avoid the risks inherent in evaluating employee traits? There are other approaches to performance appraisal which still involve some subjectivity, but provide a much sounder basis for the performance appraisal interview. They appear in columns II and III of Table 3.3. Let's consider each.

**Evaluating performance.** Employees should be evaluated in terms of *what they do, not what they are.* Appraisal methods that truly evaluate the performance of employees provide an appropriate basis for performance appraisal interviews. Of the number of methods for evaluating performance, three appear in column II of Table 3.3. Essay appraisals are most common in small organizations where the performance appraisal process is rather informal. Supervisors or managers summarize in narrative form the major responsibilities of an employee and how well he or she is performing these responsibilities. Essay appraisals are most likely to focus on performance (rather than on personal traits) when they are based on a job description that lists the main duties of a job.

Behavioral checklists are more standardized than are essay appraisals. These checklists may include between a few dozen to over a hundred specific duties for which employees are responsible. The supervisor or manager then checks each duty that the employee is performing satisfactorily, and a total score is computed to reflect the level of performance of each employee.

Behaviorally based rating scales are another example of performance appraisals. They are essentially an extension of behavioral check lists. That is, specific examples of performance are placed along the continuum of a rating scale, depending on how positive or negative those examples are. In the illustration in Table 3.5, specific examples of the performance factor being rated—*communicating*—appear next to points on the rating scale. If you compare the rating scales in Tables 3.4 and 3.5, you will find that the behaviorally based scale is superior to the trait-rating scale in three ways. First, the factor that is being evaluated is *behavioral.* The act of communicating can be directly observed rather than inferred, as is the case with a trait such as initiative. Second, the factor being evaluated is defined to minimize the possibility of different interpretations by supervisors. Third, the points on the scale, rather than being defined by vague terms like "good" or "fair," are defined by actual examples of on-the-job performance.

**TABLE 3.5**
**Behaviorally Based Rating Scale**

| | | |
|---|---|---|
| COMMUNICATING: Transmitting and receiving written and verbal information or instruction between the proper parties and following up to ensure that the message was received and understood. | | |
| High | 7 | Gives clear instructions and follows up to see that his or her people have what is needed to accomplish their job task. |
| | 6 | Passes along necessary verbal and written information based on the order of importance so that schedules will be met. |
| | 5 | Takes information as received and informs all departments that may be affected by that information. |
| Moderate | 4 | Receives instructions or information and reports back on job progress. |
| | 3 | Uses information sent to him or her, but does not relay information to other areas. |
| | 2 | Agrees to a job task without understanding what is involved and then does nothing to get the information or assistance needed to accomplish the task. |
| Low | 1 | Fails to pass information on to employees under his or her jurisdiction. |

This makes the rating scales easier for the supervisor or manager to fill out and easier for the employee to understand in a feedback session.[6]

**Evaluating results.** Another common procedure for appraising employee performance is to assess how well employees produce results. The performance appraisal interview, then, focuses on a review of past goals (were they met and why?), and the employee and his or her supervisor set new goals for the employee to achieve. These approaches (e.g., management by objectives[7] and work planning and review[8]) strive to measure employee performance in a less subjective way be establishing goals that are easily quantified. Some examples of relatively objective goals are an increase of 5 percent in sales volume, a reduction of 3 percent in turnover, or an increase of 8 percent in production.

Because such goals can be measured with precision, there is little chance for misinterpretation of the performance standard on which the performance appraisal interview is based. Sales volume either increased 5 percent or it did not. A potential problem, however, is that the goals may not fairly reflect the individual employee's performance. Goals are frequently influenced by many factors outside the control of the employee, such as economic conditions, regional variation in sales potential, and performance of other employees.

Another potential shortcoming of appraisal methods based on results arises in the nature of the feedback they provide to employees. As a supervisor, you give employees feedback to help them improve the job performance in the future. Feedback about what goals have been achieved, however, may say little to employees about what they must *do* on a day-to-day basis to improve and achieve higher goals. Goals are ends or results; performance is the means to these ends. For example, if you tell an employee that the sales quota was missed by 2 percent, this information alone is not very useful. The employee needs additional feedback about what was done on a day-to-day basis that contributed to the failure to accomplish the goal. For example, the employee may need to be told how well product knowledge was communicated, how well good relationships with customers were established and maintained, how well a sale was closed, and so forth. To be useful, feedback should focus not only on what is achieved but also on the performance that contributed to goal accomplishment. Therefore, performance appraisal interviews should contain feedback from appraisal methods from *both* columns II and III in Table 3.3 to be most useful to employees.

## MAKING FEEDBACK USEFUL

We give employees feedback to help them to improve their job performance. Another serious weakness in performance appraisal interviews is that often the feedback employees receive isn't useful to them; that is, it doesn't give them enough specific information and guidance to help them change their performance. The usefulness of the feedback is directly related to the method used to appraise performance. Useful feedback has four basic characteristics. Let's consider each of these in turn.

1. *Behavioral, not personal.* As we have already discussed, feedback should be given about what employees *do* or *achieve*, not about what they are. There are two basic reasons for this. First, personal feedback makes employees defensive. If you are filling out trait-rating scales and are consequently passing judgment on your employees' basic character, you may threaten those employees' self-esteem. If you tell an employee that he or she just doesn't have the right personality for sales, that employee is very likely to argue and claim that he or she has always been well liked and has gotten along well with people. If you rate the employee average in maturity, that employee is likely to be insulted.

A second shortcoming of personal feedback is that it is not *useful.* Employees cannot use assessments of their personal traits. Indeed, an employee may have the wrong personality for sales, but that employee has little control over his or her personality. People spend years in psychotherapy to change their personalities, and yet you're telling an employee to change his or her personality by this time next year! If, on the other hand, you tell the employee what he or she does on the job that leads you to the conclusion that his or her personality is poor or attitude is bad, the employee will find this feedback more useful. The employee has more control over how he or she behaves. If you say

> "You frown and interrupt customers when they raise reservations about our product."
>
> "You doodle and do paperwork when others are speaking in sales meetings."
>
> "You push clients too hard when trying to close a sale."

The employee can use this feedback; the employee may not like what you have said, but he or she can alter frowns, interruptions, doodling, and pressuring clients. These behaviors can be controlled, and the employee has the potential to change them.

2. *Specific, not general.* Feedback in performance appraisal interviews is often given in general terms. If you tell your employees that they are doing a good job, if you ask them to keep up the good work, or if you instruct them to give more attention to a particular area because improvement is needed, you will probably not be very successful at changing their performance. This is not because your assessments are incorrect, but this kind of feedback is too general to give employees enough detailed information about what they have done that they need to change.

Instead, you need to give your employees feedback that specifies the behaviors they need to alter on a daily or weekly basis and the behaviors they should continue to maintain at a high level. Try to make your feedback specific and behavioral; you will find that it really affects how your employees perform in the future.

One of the cruel realities of performance appraisal is that praise is often given in general terms, but criticism is almost always specific. For example, an employee may be told

> "We're very pleased with your performance in the technical area. This is a strength that's stood out in your work ever since you joined the company."

This general praise may encompass over 50 percent of the employee's job responsibilities, but it says very little about what he or she is doing well. Consider the negative feedback:

> ". . . and you simply must pay more attention to detail. Remember that shipment you sent to Birmingham, England, rather than Birmingham, Alabama? Do you realize how much that cost the company? $1,352.43! We just can't tolerate that kind of mistake."

This brings us to another characteristic of feedback.

3. *Balanced.* Because praise is typically general and criticism specific, time spent on criticism is often much greater than the time spent on praise. Many performance appraisal interviews are

characterized by a "sandwich" approach. They begin with a minute or two of general praise, followed by that telltale word "but" or "however." Then comes twenty-five minutes of discussion about problem areas and ways in which the employee needs to improve. The interview then ends with a brief dose of reassuring praise. The result is an interview in which the majority of time was spent on what the employee has done wrong. And yet that same employee may be performing acceptably well on the majority of the responsibilities which make up the job.

It is important for you to maintain a balance between positive and negative feedback in the interview. Time spent on each should roughly match the proportion of acceptable and unacceptable job performance of the employee being appraised. You will achieve a better balance in your performance appraisal interviews by giving specific, behavioral feedback about not only the job areas in which employees must improve but also the areas in which they are doing well.

4. *Future oriented.* The past is dead and should not be belabored in a performance appraisal interview. Rather, it should serve as a springboard for planning for the future. It is important, therefore, that you turn your attention to the future before you complete the interview and set some goals. And, remember, these goals are most likely to be achieved if they are *specific*. General goals such as "doing my best" or "trying harder" are less likely to lead to improved performance. Like New Year's resolutions, they are easily set and just as easily forgotten. Futhermore, general goals provide unclear targets. Employees may be highly motivated to change, but general goals like "being more cooperative," "improving my attitude," or "working harder to meet the sales quota" are too vague to specify where employees should direct their energy.

Finally, whenever possible, goals should also be mutually endorsed by both you and your employee. People tend to form a stronger commitment to goals they set for themselves than to those they are instructed to achieve. Therefore, a performance appraisal interview in which employees set their own specific goals is most likely to lead to changes in performance.

## PLANNING SUCCESSFUL PERFORMANCE APPRAISAL INTERVIEWS

So far, I have stressed what you need to do *before* the interview to make it successful. Separating the performance appraisal interview, which deals with employee development, from the salary review interview, which focuses on salary and administration, is a good beginning. In addition, in each interview you conduct, you need to concentrate on the objectives of the performance appraisal interview that are pertinent to that employee's interests and goals. Finally, the method used by your organization to appraise employee performance is crucial because it determines the nature of the feedback you give your employees during the interview. If you make the feedback useful to your employees and they see it as fair and truly representative of what they have actually done on the job, your interviews are much more likely to be successful.

## CONDUCTING THE PERFORMANCE APPRAISAL INTERVIEW

### APPROACH

Regardless of how well you have planned the interview, it will fail if you do not conduct it properly. Discovering an approach to conducting the interview that works for them often looms as a serious struggle for supervisors. Proceeding as you usually do in your daily contact with employees is not likely to work. The performance appraisal interview is *different*. It is more formal and important than the typical interactions you have with your employees.

How can you approach this troublesome interview? Norman Maier[9] identified three fundamental approaches to conducting performance appraisal interviews. Just as I have done, Maier limited the appraisal interview to those objectives which involve employee development. Consequently, his three basic approaches do not address administrative matters like salary increases or promotion.

Maier named the three approaches "tell and sell," "tell and listen," and "problem solving." The basic ingredients of each approach are outlined in Table 3.6. As you read through the following summaries of each approach, you may recognize yourself.

**Tell and sell.**  Here the supervisor's main intention is to tell employees what is right and wrong with their performance and what changes are necessary in the future. The supervisor then strives to convince the employee to accept this judgment. The supervisor assumes the role of an all-powerful and all-knowing judge of the employee and uses various persuasive and pressure techniques to get the employee to accept the judgment.

**Tell and listen.**  In this approach the supervisor also serves as a judge of employees and tells them what is right and wrong with their past performance. This approach is based on the assumption that the boss has all the answers, and, to get employees to improve their performance, he or she must merely communicate those answers to the employees. After the telling is done, however, the supervisor does not press the employee to accept this judgment, as was done in "tell and sell." Instead, the supervisor becomes very nondirective and lets the employees vent their feelings of disappointment and defensiveness. The supervisor allows the employees to complain about how they were evaluated and remains very understanding and sympathetic during this period in the interview. The assumption is that, if employees are allowed to express their feelings of disappointment and resentment, they will be more likely to accept the supervisor's judgment ultimately. Note that there is more upward communication in this interview than in "tell and sell," but the employees still contribute nothing to the supervisor's evaluation of them. The supervisor is still the all-knowing and all-powerful judge.

**Problem solving.**  In the problem-solving approach, the role of the supervisor shifts from judge to helper. The supervisor's intention is to allow employees to evaluate their own performance, identify their own problems, and set their own goals for improve-

## TABLE 3.6
### Cause-and-Effect Relations in Three Types of Appraisal Interviews[10]

| Method (Role of interviewer) | Tell and sell (Judge) | Tell and listen (Judge) | Problem solving (Helper) |
|---|---|---|---|
| Objectives | To communicate evaluation <br> To persuade E to improve | To communicate evaluation <br> To release defensive feelings | To stimulate growth and development in E |
| Assumptions | E desires to correct weaknesses if he or she knows them <br> Any person can improve if he or she so chooses <br> A superior is qualified to evaluate a subordinate | People will change if defensive feelings are removed | Growth can occur without correcting faults <br> Discussing the job problems leads to improved performance |
| Reactions | Defensive behavior suppressed <br> Attempts to cover hostility | Defensive behavior expressed <br> Person feels accepted | Problem-solving behavior |
| Skills | Selling ability <br> Patience | Listening and reflecting feelings <br> Summarizing | Listening and reflecting feelings <br> Reflecting ideas <br> Using exploratory questions <br> Summarizing |

| | | | |
|---|---|---|---|
| Attitude | People profit from criticism and appreciate help | One can respect the feelings of others if one understands them | Discussion develops new ideas and mutual interests |
| Motivation | Use of positive or negative incentives or both (extrinsic in that motivation is added to the job itself) | Resistance to change reduced<br>Passive incentive (extrinsic and some intrinsic motivation) | Increased freedom<br>Increased responsibility (intrinsic movitation in that interest is inherent in the task) |
| Gains | Success most probable when E respects interviewer | Develops favorable attitude toward superior which increases probability of success | Almost assured of improvement in some respect |
| Risks | Loss of loyalty<br>Inhibition of independent judgment<br>Face-saving problems created | Need for change may not be developed | E may lack ideas<br>Change may be other than what superior had in mind |
| Values | Perpetuates existing practices and values | Permits interviewer to change his or her views in the light of E's responses<br>Change is facilitated<br>Some upward communication | Both learn since experience and views are pooled |

ment in the future. The supervisor begins the interview by asking employees to evaluate their own performance. During this discussion the supervisor uses nondirective skills such as reflecting ideas and feelings, asking for elaboration and clarification, and summarizing to draw out the employees' ideas and evaluation. There is a strong orientation toward the future in this interview, as employees are encouraged to set goals for improved performance to identify steps necessary to meet these goals. These steps may include informal assistance from the supervisor or more formal training courses or even changes in job responsibilities.

## THE RISKS

As Maier points out, any one each of these three approaches may be appropriate for a specific employee. Young, inexperienced employees who respect their supervisor's judgment may find a tell-and-sell interview most useful for themselves. For an experienced and knowledgeable employee, a problem-solving approach may work best.

Unfortunately, however, each of these three approaches may also fail. The problem-solving approach has its pitfalls. When asked for a self-appraisal, the employee may say very little or may fail to raise the problems the supervisor wishes to address. When asked for goals, the employee may have none to offer. A second risk of the problem-solving interview is that the employee may have plenty to say, but it may not be what the supervisor wants to hear. The employee may evaluate his or her performance quite differently than the supervisor has evaluated the employee. The employee may also propose goals that the supervisor feels are inappropriate.

The tell-and-sell and tell-and-listen approaches run a particularly high risk of failure. The supervisor may be wrong in his or her appraisal of the employee. Furthermore, being told what they're doing wrong and how they must change can make employees defensive and angry. And, of course, the telling interviews reduce communication from the employee to the supervisor to a minimum and can thoroughly demoralize an employee who has something positive to contribute in the interview.

I'll illustrate the devastating effects of the tell-and-sell approach with the Burke–Stanley case included at the end of this chapter. Please read the general description of the case and the roles for Tom Burke and George Stanley and then return to the transcript.

STANLEY:    "In our interview today I'd like to outline your performance as I see it, and I'd appreciate your comments. I feel that in the technical area you've been most strong, both in creativity and originality. This has gone with you throughout your years of employment even prior to your becoming a supervisor. Productivity in your department is very high, and I feel that you are quite competent in utilizing your people to the best."

This is a typical beginning of a "telling" interview in which the boss begins with general praise and then turns to specific problems in the employee's performance.

BURKE:    "We've got a good bunch."

STANLEY:    "Good bunch, have you? I think we need to spend some time on some areas of your performance and, since we've talked about some of these things before, I don't think they'll be completely new. But I feel we should discuss them in more detail. It seems that recently you're having some problems cooperating with your fellow supervisors. There is some indication that some of the knowledge that you have is not getting to them. What do you see as the problem in that area?"

Notice that Stanley begins with a negative point and labels it a problem.

BURKE:    "Well, I think it's been pretty well proven. The more we do for them, the more they'll expect. They'll never raise their efficiency the way we have in our department. Like I said we pull together pretty well; we've got a real good crew. The fact of the matter is, the more we do for those other supervisors, the more they expect of us. I guess they're doing the best they can, but you really can't single out one department; efficiency is a plantwide thing."

STANLEY:    "But don't you think that with all the expertise and knowledge you have that you can benefit the company by helping out these other supervisors?"

BURKE:   "Well, if you're assessing the potential of the men, my young junior designer, Frank Dobbs, could probably do about any supervisory job in the place. Now there's spreading our expertise into another department if he were made supervisor."

STANLEY:   "I'm more concerned, though, Tom, with the apparent lack of co-operation between you and the other supervisors in the department and the liaison back and forth which apparently isn't there. Do you not feel that working closer with these other people would only help to improve our overall situation?"

Notice that Stanley ignores Burke's proposal to promote Dobbs and presses on with his point.

BURKE:   "Well, if you remember, I did work pretty closely with them for over a year, and I slowly had to stop it. I can only spread myself so thin. I didn't see any improvement in the other supervisors' productivity. And I do have my own department to look after."

STANLEY:   "Well, it is a problem that we're going to have to solve in one way or another. We may have to help you out with your work load, but I do feel that the contribution you can make to the department as a whole is lacking at this point. We're going to have to work very strongly on this."

Again, Stanley fails to respond to what Burke says.

STANLEY:   "Another thing that's become apparent recently has been seemingly low morale among your employees. This situation is not something I can really put my finger on, but have you noticed the problem and what do you think the reason for it is?"

The interview continues in this vein. Stanley raises additional problems of Burke's attitude, his desire to have the most interesting projects in the section assigned to his group, and his view that he is more productive than the other supervisors. Burke continues to argue or give lip service to Stanley's proposals, but there is little likelihood that Burke will perform differently next year.

Some important issues in this case must be addressed. Burke must take his share of the routine projects of the section, and all eight supervisors need to work and consult with one another more closely. Some changes are also necessary to reduce turnover in the section. How these issues are addressed, however, is crucial. With an experienced employee like Tom Burke, the tell-and-sell approach is very unlikely to be effective.

## AN ALTERNATIVE:
## PROBLEM SOLVE AND TELL

What we need is an approach to the performance appraisal interview which combines the strengths of Maier's three methods but minimizes the risks of each. My recommendation is a composite of the problem-solving and telling types of interviews. It is quite clear that beginning with a telling approach will make it almost impossible to shift in the same interview to a problem-solving approach. Once the supervisor has snuffed out an employee's attempts to be heard, it is unlikely that the employee will open up later in the interview. Therefore, I propose an interview format which begins with problem solving and then shifts to a tell if necessary. The format is shown in Table 3.7.

### BEFORE THE INTERVIEW

As a supervisor or manager, you must do your homework before the interview. You should have done an informal or formal appraisal of each of your employee's performance. You will therefore enter the interview with an agenda containing your assessment of the employee's past performance and your ideas of how he or she may change.

To maximize the upward communication in the interview, you must encourage the employee to do some homework, too. Schedule the meeting about a week ahead of time and explain its purpose to your employees. Prior to the interview, encourage them to think about two topics: (1) how well they have performed in the past year and (2) their work and career goals in the forthcoming year. What form the employees' preparation takes depends on the nature of the organization's performance appraisal system. In a system of management by objectives or work planning and review, employees will review past goals and set new

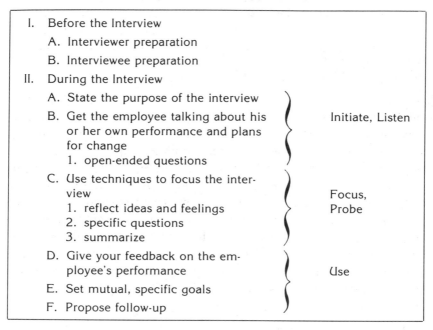

TABLE 3.7
Format of the Performance Appraisal Interview

| | |
|---|---|
| I. Before the Interview | |
|   A. Interviewer preparation | |
|   B. Interviewee preparation | |
| II. During the Interview | |
|   A. State the purpose of the interview | |
|   B. Get the employee talking about his or her own performance and plans for change<br>    1. open-ended questions | Initiate, Listen |
|   C. Use techniques to focus the interview<br>    1. reflect ideas and feelings<br>    2. specific questions<br>    3. summarize | Focus, Probe |
|   D. Give your feedback on the employee's performance | Use |
|   E. Set mutual, specific goals | |
|   F. Propose follow-up | |

goals for the future. In a system where performance is evaluated formally, employees may rate their own performance on a checklist or rating scale. Whatever the approach to performance appraisal, it is important that employees enter the interview having looked both to the past and to the future.

## DURING THE INTERVIEW

**Restate the purpose of the interview.** Simply saying that the time has come for you to meet with each of your employees to discuss how they have performed during the past year and to hear their plans for the next twelve months is a clear way to begin the interview. Some supervisors make a little small talk and then explain the purpose, but doing so depends largely on your relationship with the employee. A good rule of thumb is to begin this interview the way you begin other meetings with your employees. If you usually get right down to business, avoid small talk in the performance appraisal interview. If you usually chat informally for a few minutes, do so in this interview.

**Get your employee talking.** As a supervisor or manager, you have the responsibility of evaluating your employees' performance as well as helping them to improve. You will enter the interview with an agenda. You will have already completed an evaluation of the employee's performance, and you will have identified areas of work where the employee is effective and areas in which you feel improvement is needed. Your goals in this early stage of the interview are to get the employee to *raise and add to your agenda* and to *learn* as much as possible *about why the employee is performing* as he or she is. To achieve these goals you need to begin the sequence for conducting the interview: initiate, listen, focus, probe, use.

You will have already initiated the discussion when you schedule the interview and ask the employee to do some thinking about past performance and future goals. To begin this stage of the interview, you ask an open-ended question such as

"How would you assess your own performance over this past year?"

or

"What goals do you feel you have achieved during this past year?"

or

"What achievements have given you a particular sense of satisfaction at work during the last twelve months?"

As the employee responds, you need to listen very carefully for points you wish to follow up on.

**Use techniques to focus the interview.** Here is where the tone of the interview is set. You must resist the temptation to jump to the "telling" portion of the interview or to focus only on your agenda items. You must be patient and dig for what the employee has to contribute. If, for example, an employee's answer to the first question is, "I think I've done fine," the ball is very abruptly back in your court. You must come back with a more specific question to keep the employee talking. For example, "Well, I'm pleased to hear that you feel that way. Can you name some of the things you've done that you are particularly pleased with?"

As the employee raises topics, you must store them in your memory and bring each up for discussion. Let's consider, for example, the case of Tom Burke and George Stanley. Suppose Burke raises his success in training and developing his employees, the technical performance of his group, and his concern about his relationship with the other supervisors. When an employee raises a number of issues, begin by focusing on a positive one. Avoid the trap of jumping on Tom's problems with the other supervisors as soon as it is raised. Focus on an issue by reflecting or using a specific question. For example,

> "So you feel you've been particularly successful this last year in developing your juniors."

or

> "You mentioned how well your group has produced this past year. What do you feel you've done to make the group effective?"

Notice in the second example that the specific question focuses on what Tom has done, how he has performed, to contribute to the group's effectiveness. It's important to get down to specific performance.

When you address problem areas, you are likely to encounter some strong feelings. *A rule of thumb is to deal with the feelings first.* Consider the problem of lack of cooperation between Tom Burke and the other seven supervisors. Let's say that Tom alludes to this problem and that his boss, George Stanley, raises it in the following way:

STANLEY:   "I gather from what you said earlier, Tom, that there's been little change in your working relationship with the other supervisors."

BURKE:  "If anything, it's worse. These guys will hardly talk to me anymore!"

STANLEY:  "You don't sound very happy about it."

BURKE:  "Well, I'm not. It really bugs me when the deadwood around here just leans on me."

STANLEY:  "Pretty frustrating situation, that's for sure."

BURKE:  "Hell yes. I think we should fire the whole bunch of them!"

STANLEY:  "It seems as though you're about at the end of your rope."

BURKE:  "Well, I am. I just don't know what else can be done."

STANLEY:  "I know the feeling, Tom. I feel as if I've been banging my head against a wall, struggling with this thing, too. Let's start at the beginning. Give me your view of what has happened in the last year that has contributed to the problem."

Notice that Stanley shows awareness of the pain and frustration that Burke is experiencing and gives him an opportunity to vent those feelings before taking a rational, less emotional look. Burke has said, in exasperation, some things he probably doesn't really mean. It is crucial that Stanley not lecture or scold Burke about his feelings. For example, after their first exchange, Stanley would make a mistake if he embarked on a lecture about how communication and cooperation are essential. Similarly, when Burke refers to his colleagues as "deadwood" and proposes that they be fired, Stanley must avoid scolding Burke for making such comments about them. Doing so at this time would only push Burke into a corner and force him to defend statements he probably doesn't fully endorse. Emphasis in this part of the interview is on collecting information from the employee. The interviewer should do as little telling as possible.

I want to be clear here. Supervisors should not necessarily avoid confrontations in the performance appraisal interview. For example, if Burke still endorses these views and proposals regarding his colleagues even after he has vented his emotions, Stanley must state clearly that he does not agree. But the timing is crucial. Disagreements early in the interview will likely succeed only in reducing communication. This point is illustrated well in the contrast between the excerpt from a tell-and-sell interview presented earlier in this chapter and the interview transcript that appears at the end of the chapter. In the short tell-and-sell excerpt, Stanley completely ignores Burke's feelings and proposals and essentially lectures Burke, but this approach leads to no clear solution. In the interview transcript at the end of the chapter, however, Stanley responds to the feelings, and the two men develop some ideas to remedy the problem.

**Give feedback on employee performance.**    To this point the interview has the character of Maier's problem-solving approach. This phase of the interview may last only a few minutes with some employees and perhaps an hour with others. By beginning this way, you are allowing for as much upward communication as possible. There are some risks to this approach, however. Employees may have little to say about their performance, or their own evaluations may differ significantly from the supervisor's appraisal. Finally, they may not raise the topics on your agenda.

The next stage of the interview, therefore, is designed for you to do some telling. It is important to note, however, that this telling follows a period of discussion of the employee's topics. Consequently, the employee is now likely to be receptive to your views. There may be some specific topics which you planned to raise during the interview that were not raised by the employee; this is the time to bring those topics up. If you have done ratings or some other form of written evaluation, this is the time to show them to the employee. I wish to stress that, as soon as you place an evaluation form on the desk or refer to it, the interview becomes a "telling" interview. Once the telling phase begins, it is almost impossible to change to the problem-solving approach with its emphasis on upward communication. Therefore, you must avoid the temptation to begin the interview with a discussion of your ratings of employee performance. In fact, you may learn something in the first phase of the interview which influences you to revise your ratings.

**Set mutual, specific goals.**    On the basis of discussion to this point, you and your employee should set some goals which are as specific as possible and are ideally endorsed by both parties. Some of these goals may have already emerged in the earlier discussion, but at this time they should be restated and recorded.

**Propose follow-up.**  Plans for change, like New Year's resolutions, may be made in the fervor of the moment and quickly forgotten. It is very useful to conclude the interview by setting the timing and nature of the follow-up to monitor the employee's proposed goals. Through follow-up you can also assess whether the goals are appropriate or feasible. If, for example, an employee sets a goal that is not compatible with company policy or is beyond the employee's personal capabilities, quick follow-up will enable you and your employee to revise the goal.

## INTERVIEW STYLE, SUPERVISORY STYLE, AND ORGANIZATION CLIMATE

As with all interviews covered in this book, the approach I recommend includes a good degree of flexibility, and you must tailor it to your own personal style and organization. You must conduct the performance appraisal interview in a way that is consistent with your style of supervision. For example, the autocrat who tries to adopt the problem solve-and-tell approach will be viewed with suspicion and even disbelief by employees. Such a boss may be better off with a tell-and-sell approach. If you practice a consultative or participative style of management, however, you will find my approach to the interview quite compatible.

How successfully you implement the principles of this chapter will also be strongly influenced by the recent history of performance appraisal in your organization. Most organizations need to revise their methods of appraising performance; most evaluate people, not performance. Moreover, many managers and supervisors conduct "telling" interviews because they perceive their role as judge. Employees learn to mistrust this kind of performance appraisal system, and overcoming that negative climate will take time. Developing a new method of evaluating performance is an essential first step. Next, the salary review and performance appraisal should be split and covered in two distinct interviews. Third, as managers and supervisors, you need to alter your approach to conducting the interview so that two-way communication is achieved. If you are able to take these steps in your organization, performance appraisal can contribute to the positive development of employees and ultimately to the effectiveness of the organization.

## INTERVIEW TRANSCRIPT

This section contains a transcript of a performance appraisal interview conducted with the problem solve-and-tell approach. The interview is based on a case[11] involving George Stanley, a section head in the engineering department of a construction company, and Tom Burke, a supervisor who reports to Stanley. The transcript is based on an actual interview which was conducted with the Stanley–Burke role playing exercise. As a role play, it is not as detailed or complex as performance appraisal interviews you might conduct with actual employees. The interview does illustrate, however, how strongly the approach to the interview influences the response of the employee and the outcome of the discussion.

### GENERAL INSTRUCTIONS

George Stanley is the electrical section head in the Engineering Department of the American Construction Company. The work in the department includes design, drafting, cost estimates, keeping maps up to date, checking standards and building codes, field inspection and follow-up, and so on. Eight first-line supervisors report to George Stanley. The duties of the supervisors are partly technical and partly supervisory. The organizational chart for Mr. Stanley's section is as shown.

Company policy requires that all section heads interview each of their supervisors once a year, the purpose being

1. to evaluate the supervisor's performance during the year,
2. to give recognition for jobs well done, and
3. to correct weaknesses.

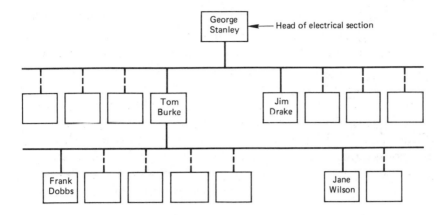

The company believes that employees should know how they stand and that everything should be done to develop management personnel. The evaluation interviews were introduced to serve this purpose.

Tom Burke is one of the supervisors reporting to Stanley; today we will witness an evaluation interview conducted by Stanley with Tom Burke.

Tom Burke has a college degree in electrical engineering and in addition to his technical duties, which often take him to the field, he supervises the work of one junior designer, six draftsmen, and two women clerks. He is highly paid as are all of the supervisors in this department because of the high requirements in technical knowledge. Burke has been with the company for twelve years and has been a supervisor for two years. He is married and has two children. He owns his home and is active in the civic affairs of the community in which he lives.

## ROLE FOR GEORGE STANLEY, SECTION HEAD

You have evaluated all of the supervisors who report to you and during the next two weeks will interview each of them. You hope to use these interviews constructively to develop each man. Today you have arranged to interview Tom Burke, one of the eight first-line supervisors who report to you. Here is the information and his evaluation as given in your files.

Thomas Burke: twelve years with the company, two years as supervisor, college degree, married, two children. Evaluation: Highly creative and original and exceptionally competent technically. His unit is very productive and during the two years he supervised the group there has been a steady improvement. Within the past six months you have given him extra work and he has gotten this done on schedule. As far as productivity and dependability are concerned, he is your top man.

His cooperation with other supervisors in the section leaves much to be desired. Before you made him a supervisor, his originality and technical knowledge were available to your whole section. Gradually he has withdrawn and now acts more as a lone wolf. You've asked other supervisors to talk over certain problems with him but they tell you he offers no suggestions. He tells them he's busy or listens disinterestedly to their problems, kids them, or makes sarcastic remarks, depending on his mood. On one occasion he allowed Jim Drake, one of the supervisors in another unit, to make a mistake that he could have forestalled by letting him know the status of certain design changes which he knew about and had seen. It is to be expected that supervisors cooperate on matters involving design changes that affect them.

Furthermore, during the past six months he has been unwilling to take two assignments. He said they were routine, that he preferred more interesting work, and he advised you to give the assignments to other supervisors. To prevent trouble, you followed his suggestion. However, you feel that you can't give him all of the interesting work and that if he persists in this attitude there will be trouble. You cannot play favorites and keep up morale in your unit.

Burke's failure to cooperate has you worried for another reason. Although his group is highly productive, there is more turnover among his draftsmen than in other groups. You have heard no complaints as yet, but you suspect that he may be treating his men in an arbitrary manner. Certainly if he talks up to you and other supervisors, he's likely to be even more that way with his men. Apparently the high productivity in his group is not due to high morale but to his ability to use his men to do the things for which they are best suited. This method won't develop good draftsmen. You hope to discuss these matters with Burke in such a way as to recognize his good points and at the same time correct some of his weaknesses.

## ROLE FOR TOM BURKE, SUPERVISOR

One junior designer, six draftsmen, and two women clerks report to you. You feel that you get along fine with your group. You have always been pretty much of an idea man and apparently have the knack of passing on your enthusiasm to others in your group. There is a lot of "we" feeling in your unit because it is obvious that your group is the most productive.

You believe in developing your men and always give them strong recommendations. You feel you have gained the reputation of developing your employees because they frequently go out and get much better jobs. Since promotion is necessarily slow in a company such as yours, you feel that the best way to stimulate morale is to develop new men and demonstrate that a good man can get somewhere. The two girls in your unit are bright and efficient and there is a lot of good-natured kidding. Recently one of your girls, Jane Wilson, turned down an outside offer that paid $95 a month more, for she preferred to stay in your group. You are going to get her a raise the first chance you have.

The other supervisors in George Stanley's section do not have your enthusiasm. Some of them are dull and unimaginative. During your first year as supervisor you used to help them a lot, but you soon found that they leaned on you and before long you were doing their work. There is a lot of pressure to get out production. You got your promotion by producing and you don't intend to let other supervisors interfere. Since you no longer help the other supervisors your production has gone up, but a couple of them seem a bit sore at you. Frank, your junior designer, is a better man than most of them and you'd like to see him made a supervisor. Since the company has some deadwood in it, Stanley ought to recognize this fact and assign to such units the more routine jobs. Then they wouldn't need your help and you could concentrate your efforts on jobs that suit your unit. At present, George Stanley passes out work pretty much as he gets it. Because you are efficient you get more than your share of these jobs, and you see no reason why the extra work shouldn't be in the form of "plums." This would motivate units to turn out work. When you suggested to Stanley that he turn over some of the more routine jobs to other supervisors he did it, but he sure was reluctant about it.

You did one thing recently that has bothered you. There was a design change in a set of plans and you should have told Jim Drake (a fellow supervisor) about it, but it slipped your mind. Drake was out when you had it on your mind and then you got involved in a hot idea that Frank, your junior designer, had and forgot all about the matter with Drake. As a result, Drake had to make a lot of unnecessary changes and he was quite sore about it. You told him you were sorry and offered to make the changes, but he turned down the offer.

Today you have an interview with George Stanley. It's about this management development plan in the company. It shouldn't take very long, but it's nice to have the boss tell you about the job you are turning out. Maybe there is a raise in it; maybe he'll tell you something about what to expect in the future.

STANLEY:   "As I said last week when we set up this appointment, Tom, this is our annual performance review meeting. I'd like to get your views on your performance over the past year and discuss your plans for the upcoming year."

BURKE:   "Fine, that sounds good to me."

STANLEY:   "I'm glad to hear you feel that way, Tom. I'd like to begin by asking you how you would evaluate your performance over this past year."

Stanley invites Burke to volunteer his views.

BURKE:   "Well, George, I feel it's been a pretty good year, all things considered."

STANLEY:  "So you feel generally satisfied, then. Is there anything that stands out in your mind?"

BURKE:  "I'm particularly pleased with the group reporting to me. They're a really good bunch and we pull together real well."

STANLEY:  "You sound really excited about your group, Tom. What kinds of things have you been doing to make the group effective?"

## Stanley probes for specifics about Burke's performance.

BURKE:  I've always been very enthusiastic about the technical nature of this work, and my enthusiasm rubs off on them. I also believe very strongly in developing my people. I give them all the challenge and attention they need, and it's really paying off."

STANLEY:  "Certainly the productivity of your group attests to the high-quality performance of your people, Tom. I appreciate the way you've handled the extra work I've given you in the last few months. How are your people reacting to the workload?"

BURKE:  "They thrive on it. I like to give my people the opportunity to prove themselves. I spend a lot of my time on the floor training and teaching them so they develop to the best of their ability."

STANLEY:  "You really seem excited about that part of your work, Tom."

BURKE:  "I love it. There's nothing I enjoy more than seeing my people develop and progress in their careers. I've got a junior designer, Frank Dobbs, who's ready for a promotion right now. Unfortunately, promotion is so slow in the company that I've lost a lot of people in the last year."

## Stanley probes into what Burke is doing well to maintain balance in the interview. When Burke volunteers a problem area, Stanley focuses on it carefully.

STANLEY:  "I am aware of your turnover figures."

BURKE:  "George, we've got to do something about the lack of promotion in the department. I hate to lose such fine employees."

STANLEY:  "I share your frustration about the turnover, Tom. Perhaps I could go to the personnel department and see if we can develop some more opportunities internally. What do you think?"

BURKE:  "That sounds like a good idea."

STANLEY:  "Then I'll follow up on it and get back to you in the next few weeks. We've got to keep the turnover down. What else did you want to talk about today, Tom?"

## Stanley summarizes the goal and proposes follow-up.

BURKE: "Well, it's getting more and more difficult to keep my group's production up with the heavy work load. A number of the other supervisors are coming to me with technical questions, and they're eating up huge chunks of my time. I just can't drop everything and help them out every time they come around with a problem."

STANLEY: "You sound pretty exasperated. I gather there's been little change in your working relationship with the other supervisors."

BURKE: "If anything, it's worse. These guys will hardly talk to me anymore. I tried to apologize to Jim Drake about a mixup in communication, but he wouldn't even accept my apology."

STANLEY: "You don't sound very happy about it."

BURKE: "Well, I'm not. It really bugs me when the deadwood around here just leans on me."

STANLEY: "Pretty frustrating situation, that's for sure."

BURKE: "I think we should fire the whole bunch of them!"

STANLEY: "It seems as though you're about at the end of your rope."

BURKE: "Well, I am. I just don't know what else can be done."

STANLEY: "I know the feeling, Tom. I feel as if I've been banging my head against a wall, struggling with this thing, too. Let's start at the beginning. Give me your view of what has happened in the last year that has contributed to the problem."

## Stanley acknowledges Burke's strong feelings before asking for a rational analysis of the problem.

BURKE: "As you know, I've always been pretty good technically, and, before I became a supervisor, I used to consult with several supervisors on technical problems. Well, when I became a supervisor they continued to come to me for technical help. At first I spent a lot of time with them, but my own work started piling up. I never thought this new job would demand so much of my time. So I started cutting back on the help I gave to the other supervisors. Of course, they weren't too happy about that, and some hard feelings have developed on both sides. That's about where it stands now."

STANLEY:   "You mentioned that problem with Jim Drake a minute ago."

BURKE:   "Oh, that. That was just an oversight on my part. I just forgot to get back to Jim; it was purely unintentional. But he took it the wrong way, and I got labeled as a lone wolf again."

STANLEY:   "I'm glad to hear that you didn't do it intentionally, Tom. It does seem as though we do have some communication problems around here."


## Stanley probes Burke's ideas before stating his own views.


BURKE:   "Yes, we really do keep to ourselves quite a bit. Maybe we should have a meeting to hash all of this out."

STANLEY:   "Good idea, Tom. Perhaps we could meet regularly for a while and see how it goes."

BURKE:   "Sounds good to me. There's a lot of room for improvement."

STANLEY:   "Let's try a Monday morning meeting each week for two months and then reassess the whole idea. We could use the meetings to make plans for joint efforts on work for that week. We might also work out a schedule each week for job assignments."

BURKE:   "Oh, I thought you'd bring that up today."

STANLEY:   "Yes, I want to discuss it with you, Tom. On a couple of occasions you have turned down assignments. What was your thinking at the time, Tom?"


## Stanley brings up a problem but not in a threatening way.


BURKE:   "They were routine jobs that any supervisor in the plant could handle. It seems fair to me that the most productive group in the plant should get the most interesting assignments."

STANLEY:   "Let's consider that for a minute, Tom. If I give your group the most interesting and challenging assignments, how am I going to develop the other groups so they can also handle the challenge?"

BURKE:   "I don't think they're up to the challenge. Right now, they bring their most difficult work to me, so I end up doing the work anyway. You might as well assign it to me directly."

STANLEY:   "But you've already said that you're overloaded, Tom. Your group just can't take on all the difficult jobs in the department."

BURKE:   "No, not all of them."

Burke and Stanley disagree, but neither is lecturing or threatening the other.

STANLEY:   "I need to make my position very clear, Tom. I need to develop and follow a fair system of assigning work to each group. I simply cannot give you the most interesting work, Tom. Favoring your group hurts morale and also contributes nothing to the development of technical expertise in the other groups. As I was saying before, we might work out job assignments in weekly meetings. At least then we could try to accommodate your preferences as well as everybody else's."

Stanley does some telling in a reasonable and straightforward way.

BURKE:   "We can at least give it a try."

STANLEY:   "Let's do that and then review the method of assignment after two months. To summarize, then, we set the goal of weekly meetings to promote more cooperation between groups and to work out job assignments. You've also set the goal of continuing to develop your people and trying to find other positions within the company for promotion. I'll tell you what I learn from the personnel department within the next month. Is there anything else you wish to discuss?"

BURKE:   "No. That covers my agenda for today."

STANLEY:   "I want to thank you, Tom, for a most constructive discussion. I feel that your work has been generally quite good this past year, and I feel that, if I can get all eight supervisors communicating and cooperating more effectively, then your performance will improve and so will the department's overall effectiveness."

Burke and Stanley have had a productive and nonthreatening discussion. They discussed all the topics addressed in the case without defensiveness and lecturing.

# 4

# *Counseling Interviewing*

Virtually all of us have at times struggled with a problem we were unable to solve ourselves and have turned to someone else for help. Often we may not have even been able to say with any precision what the problem was, but we knew we had strong feelings of frustration, pain, anger, or anxiety. This turning for help leads to a counseling interview. A counseling interview is a discussion between two people in which one is asking the other for assistance with a problem or predicament.

Of all the interviews addressed in this book, the counseling interview is most likely to be unplanned and unstructured, and it probably requires the highest degree of sensitivity from the interviewer. Indeed, we may not even know when we are likely to enter into such an interview. One of my early experiences back when I was doing university teaching occurred when a student asked to meet with me in my office after class. I assumed that this was going to be a typical discussion about class assignments or the nature of the course, but a couple of minutes after the student sat down the tears started to flow and she began to speak of her concern with her career plans. I found myself in the role of a counselor. Really, the counseling interview is best defined by the roles two people assume—one is willing to open up and reveal feelings and problems and the other is willing to listen and try to help.

It is important to note that most people who assume the role of counselor are not professionally trained. Social workers, psychologists, and psychiatrists are all experts in the helping professions. They counsel people who have serious personality problems or who have major difficulties in coping with everyday life. Most of you who are reading this chapter, however, are part-time counselors, just as I was when the student entered my office. As such, you must be aware of your limitations as well as your capabilities. There is much that you can do as a part-time counselor, but you must know when you are over your head and need to refer a client to a professional.

The distinction between part-time and professional counseling is determined by two factors: the setting in which the problem originates and the nature of the problem. While these two factors are clearly related, let's consider them one at a time. The setting of problems addressed in the counseling interview by managers, supervisors, or peers is work. The problems are generally work-related, such as matters of performance on the job, job or career choice, compatibility in a work group, or working conditions (travel, long hours). These are clearly work-related matters that may be appropriately discussed by another employee assuming the role of part-time counselor. Problems whose primary setting is outside of work, such as personal problems, are best left to professional counselors.

There are problems that have their roots outside the work setting but strongly influence job performance. Personal crises such as marital separation, financial stress, or problem drinking are examples. Should the part-time counselor get involved with such problems that span both the work and the home settings? Here is where the nature of the problem becomes the determining factor. Consider the instance where the wife's recent promotion conflicts with a planned transfer which will keep the husband on the fast track of career development. This problem, while involving both work and home life, could be addressed effectively in a counseling interview by many managers. On the other hand, more severe personal crises such as marital separation or problem drinking are likely beyond the expertise of even the most skillful part-time counselor and should therefore be referred to a professional.

## HELP IS A SCARCE COMMODITY

Many authors have concluded that help from a fellow human being is scarce these days. There is a reluctance for people to "get involved" in the personal business of others. We are often prone to shy away from people who are behaving unusually or appear distressed. We feel that we may be intruding.

On the other hand, those who are feeling the distress may wonder why no one takes notice. They may conclude that nobody cares enough about them to inquire and try to help. People often cry out for help in subtle and indirect ways. Many of us either do not detect the signals that people use to ask for help or we choose to ignore them.

One of the reasons that people do not ask for help more directly is in part a function of our North American culture. This is particularly true in the business world. Competence is highly valued in most organizations, as well it should be. But this emphasis on competence can be so strong that employees feel it is a liability for them not to have all the answers. How risky is it for a middle manager with twenty years of experience to admit to a work-related problem? Can the fast-track MBA afford to reveal concern over a career choice?

Whether employees in an organization can ask their peers or managers for help depends on two factors. The first is the way in which any given peer or manager views the counseling process. Does this person see it as a constructive step or an admission of weakness? The second factor is the skill of the people who conduct counseling interviews. This is probably more important than the first factor. How the counseling is actually done says much more to employees than a manager's announced views. We have all known managers who claimed that the door was always open, but they were so insensitive and unskillful in dealing with employee problems that no one ventured through the door more than once.

In this chapter I will provide guidance in how to conduct effective counseling interviews. Much of the emphasis will be on what the counselor must do, but I have included several techniques and illustrations that will also guide the client—the person who is seeking help.

## OBJECTIVES

The counseling interview is usually unplanned and unscheduled. What begins as a casual conversation or a discussion of another matter may evolve into a counseling interview. The fact that it is unplanned, however, does not mean that it has to be unstructured. As prospective counselors, you need to know the content of the typical counseling interview in order to conduct this type of interview effectively when the need arises. As always, we will begin our discussion of content with objectives.

The counseling interview has four fundamental objectives. They are

1. *Problem definition*—Promoting maximum flow of information from the client to define the problem.
2. *Problem solving*—Considering alternative solutions.
3. *Action planning*—Selecting a course of action endorsed by client and counselor.
4. *Assigning responsibility for action*—Clarifying client's commitment to change.

There are some fundamental points about these objectives which are crucial to effective counseling interviewing. First, you must address these objectives in order. A problem cannot be solved until it has been defined. While this point is obvious, there are many traps which you can fall into which shift the interview to problem solving before the problem has been clearly defined *by the client.* One common example is that many of us, when presented with a matter that is troubling a friend or acquaintance, want to relieve that person's discomfort as quickly as possible. We may also feel a strong urge to reduce our own discomfort, which develops when someone we care about is suffering. Consequently, we rush to a solution for the problem as we perceive it. This solution, however, may be premature or even inappropriate. This is just one of several examples of how counselors upset the order of these four objectives discussed more extensively later in the chapter.

A second fundamental point about these objectives is that all four must be achieved for the client to reap the most benefit possible from the interview. Many counseling interviewers complete only the first two objectives and perhaps a portion of the third. While it is true that some people face more problems than others, it is also true that some people seem always to be unhappy and are continually struggling with some form of problem. You need to be on your guard for this kind of client. They are unlikely to address all four objectives in a counseling interview. Some may define the problem and drink in all the empathy and understanding you can muster but avoid attempts to consider alternative solutions. Others may discuss alternative solutions but never set out specific plans to solve the problem. Still others will not accept responsibility for the proposed course of action but, rather, will press *you* for a solution and, if it is not successful, will blame you. You need a high degree of skill to avoid falling into the traps that clients may set either deliberately or unintentionally.

## INTERACTION OF COUNSELOR AND CLIENT

In the interview the counselor and client interact, and consequently each influences the behavior of the other. Each has basic values and feelings that contribute to his or her perceptions of the specific problem under discussion and the counseling interview in general. This interaction is shown in Figure 4.1.

The interaction of these feelings, values, and perceptions will strongly influence the approach taken in the interview and its actual outcome. I alluded earlier to the cultural value that people who seek help are weak. Managers who subscribe to this value may develop strong negative feelings toward a client. Feelings of

FIGURE 4.1
Interaction of Counselor and Client

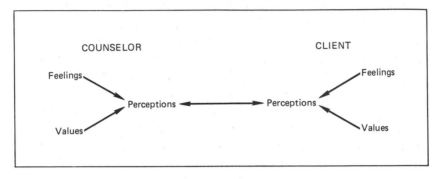

annoyance or even contempt may arise in these managers when their help is sought. They may also experience conflicting feelings if a person whom they hold in very high regard appears in the office and reveals a problem he or she cannot solve alone. Managers in these circumstances may deny the existence of the problem or try to come up with a quick solution to escape from such an uncomfortable situation.

Other people who may be called upon to conduct counseling interviews may place a high value on helping others. Earlier in this chapter I gave the example of people who gain great satisfaction from reducing the discomfort of someone who is wrestling with a problem. As counselors, these people may identify very strongly with the client's problem even before it is defined and rush to a solution by giving advice. They may leave the interview with a warm glow of satisfaction, but the client's problem may not have been addressed thoroughly.

Of course, the client's feelings and values also strongly influence the way in which the counseling interview is conducted and its outcome. Clients frequently have strong feelings of fear, frustration, or anger that distort their perceptions of the problem and potential solutions. As counselors, you must be very skillful in dealing with these feelings and perceptions. Clients may also subscribe to the value that seeking help is a sign of weakness and may therefore be experiencing a great deal of conflict when they actually ask you for help. They may be fearful and embarrassed but also sufficiently concerned about their circumstances to ask for help. As a result of this conflict, they may not be very open in the interview, showing a reluctance to own up to the problem or to give all their views and feelings. You will need to deal with this reluctance effectively if the interview is to succeed.

## APPROACH

Now let's turn to approach. Certainly the interaction of the counselor and client and the role that each assumes in the interview will determine how the interview can be approached and conducted. But you must strive to develop an approach that will not be restricted by the client's behavior. Your approach must be flexible enough to adjust to the client as well as to the problem under discussion.

Probably the most common approach to the counseling interview is that advocated by Carl Rogers[1] in client-centered therapy, that is, the nondirective approach. In its purest form the nondirective aproach involves the counselor's acting as a mirror to a client. He or she reflects the ideas or content of what the client is saying as well as the feelings that the client is expressing. The primary objective of the nondirective counselor is to help clients gain awareness of their own ideas and feelings regarding a problem. Armed with this awareness, clients then proceed to gain insight and solve their own problems.

At the other end of the continuum is the directive approach. Here the counselor diagnoses the client's problem with minimal assistance from the client and gives advice to alleviate the problem. Although the directive approach is seldom seen in a pure form, it is mostly likely to occur when there is a large difference in status and power between the client and counselor. Highly directive approaches are common between parent and child, teacher and student, and even supervisor and employee.

It is my view that neither extreme, directive or nondirective, is appropriate in the counseling interview. Rather, as counselors you must tailor your approach to your clients as well as to yourselves. Most significantly, you must tailor your approach to the objective you are dealing with in the interview.

**Begin with a nondirective approach.** The first objective—problem definition—requires a nondirective approach. It is imperative that you listen, probe, and reflect to keep the lines of communication wide open during the initial stage of the interview. It is difficult, however, for some counselors to remain nondirective until the problem has been well defined. Instead, they are prone to give in to their own needs or to rush to a solution for the problem to relieve their own discomfort or that of the client. It is necessary for you to resist these needs and maintain a nondirective approach until the client has defined the problem clearly and completely.

Strict adherence to the nondirective approach beyond the point of problem definition, however, can be not only annoying to the client but unproductive. A friend of mine once demonstrated this point with an incident from his years in a doctoral program in management. He and his fellow students were well acquainted with various counseling techniques from their graduate course work. So, when he called upon a friend for some help with a problem he had been thinking about and wrestling with for a number of days, he received only nondirective responses in return. Finally in frustration he said, "Don't give me all that nondirective stuff. I've got the problem well defined; what I need from you is ideas!"

**Become more directive as the interview progresses.** The objectives of problem solving, action planning, and assigning responsibility for action require you to give a combination of nondirective and directive responses. In general, you will need to become more directive when addressing these three objectives than when dealing with the first objective—problem definition. For example, you must help the client focus on important topics. This may require you to point out central themes in what the client has been saying and to focus the client's attention on these themes. You may also become more directive by contributing your own ideas regarding options open to the client as the interview turns to problem solving or action planning. Finally, you may need to be directive to keep the client moving through all four objectives as the interview progresses.

## FORMAT

The counseling interview is the most spontaneous and least structured of all the interviews addressed in this book. In spite of this, it has a basic format which you should follow as you find yourselves in a counseling situation. Here is the format.

**Keep the client talking.** The client will trigger the beginning of the counseling interview by asking for assistance or by revealing some need for assistance. As the counseling interviewer, your emphasis early in the interview is to keep the lines of communication wide open and to keep the client talking about the nature of the problem. Using nondirective techniques such as reflecting ideas and feelings, summarizing, and asking specific questions will keep the information flowing.

**Get the client to consider alternative solutions.** After the problem and its potential causes have been identified, your next step is to encourage the client to begin helping himself or herself. What solutions have been tried? What ideas have been considered and discarded? Here you are essentially getting the client to think aloud and consider what is possible.

**Add your own ideas.** As you and the client progress in the problem-solving stage of the interview, you may wish to offer your own alternatives for the client's consideration. I recommend that you do so cautiously and only *after* you have exhausted the client's own ideas.

**Set specific plans.** At this stage of the interview, you must help the client plan for the future. Some clients may do this automatically; others will need encouragement and direction from you. First, the client must select from among the alternatives identified in the previous two steps. Second, he or she must set out a specific plan of action which will lead to a desired change in the current predicament. You may have to use some specific questions to get the client to begin planning. "I think you have your options well in mind. What do you plan to do?" or "I think it's important that you proceed with a plan. What would you like to do next?" are good examples.

**Gain client commitment to change.** Before you end the counseling interview, you should see to it that the client clearly perceives his or her responsibility in bringing about change. In many cases individuals contribute to their own difficulties either by behaving in ways that are directly harmful to themselves or by failing to act in ways that would rid them of their difficulties. We all contribute in some way to our own problems, even if it is just by remaining in the situation which we find problematic. Consequently, we must *act* in order to solve our problems, for they are seldom resolved by the actions of others. As counselors, you must ensure that the client is aware of and accepts his or her responsibility to follow up on the plans for change to see that change does indeed occur.

## A NOTE OF CAUTION

Early in this chapter I stressed the distinction between professional counselors and the rest of us who venture into counseling only at the invitation of someone with whom we work or live. As part-time counselors, you must be aware of your limitations. In particular, you must be on the lookout for problems that you have neither the knowledge nor the skill to address effectively.

Turning to the format just discussed, I would suggest that after you have completed the first step and done your best to help the client define the problem, ask yourself, *"Can I help with this problem?"*

For example, if one of your best employees has just traced his decrease in job performance to a marital or a drinking problem, you're probably in over your head. While you may have great concern for the employee's well-being and strong views on the reason for his problems, you are very likely not the best person to serve as his counselor. It is important that you realize this *immediately* after defining the problem rather than after you have struggled further into the interview. I suggest that you state clearly that you appreciate the employee's candor and that you feel he needs more expert help than you can give. Your problem solving should then focus on identifying a more appropriate source of help for the client.

## CONDUCTING THE COUNSELING INTERVIEW

Now that we have set out a format to meet the objectives of the counseling interview, let's turn to the art of conducting this kind of interview. The counseling interview is different from the other five interview types discussed in this book. In each of the other five, interviewers have a set of objectives, a format, *and an agenda of topics* they wish to cover. As counseling interviewers, you also have objectives and a format, but you have no preplanned agenda of topics. Consequently, in the counseling interview you must work exclusively with the material raised by the client. To use what the client is saying as effectively as possible, you must rely heavily on the sequence of initiate–listen–focus–probe–use. Following this sequence will help you to minimize the influence of your own views in the counseling interview and to maintain a predominantly nondirective approach. Let's consider this sequence in more detail.

Initiate.   There are two ways in which to initiate a counseling interview. The first is for the manager, supervisor, or colleague of the prospective client to take the initiative by assuming the role of the counseling interviewer and inviting the other person to assume the role of the client. Initiating the interview this way is risky and requires a great deal of sensitivity. I recommend that you use this method only with people with whom you have already established a good relationship. Begin by describing the changes you have observed in the individual's behavior and then express your willingness to help. For example,

COUNSELOR:   "I've noticed a change in your work schedule in the past couple of weeks. You've been coming in later and leaving earlier than I've seen you do in the three years you've been in the department. I've been scratching my head and thinking that this just isn't like you. In the past I've always been able to count on coming in to a hot pot of coffee that you've started an hour earlier. I just want you to know that if you'd like to talk, I'd be pleased to listen."

CLIENT:  "Well, I have been stewing about something and I guess it shows. You remember that promotion I applied for? They turned me down and brought in someone from outside the company."

It's important that you not deal in vague generalities when trying to initiate the interview. Say in specific terms what you have observed and express your willingness to help.

The second way to initiate a counseling interview is to respond to another employee's request for assistance or expression of negative feelings. Here you are responding to a prospective client's direct or subtle invitation to assume the role of counselor. Sometimes the invitation is quite straightforward, as in the following example.

CLIENT:  "I'd like to talk with you about a job change I've been considering. I've been wrestling with it for a couple of weeks now, and I'd really appreciate your thoughts."

COUNSELOR:  "I'd be happy to help if I can. Can you just start at the beginning?"

Frequently, however, the call for help is indirect. In these cases you have to be quite sensitive to the feelings that accompany the employee's words and if you sense a good deal of distress, reflect the feelings. For example,

CLIENT:  "Another meeting where all we talk about is budget cuts and how we can adjust to them. This department is going down hill fast."

COUNSELOR:  "It is a pretty discouraging situation, isn't it."

CLIENT:  "Now that's an understatement. I'm about to pull out my resumé and update it."

COUNSELOR:  "It sounds like this place is really getting you down. Would you like to talk it over?"

CLIENT:  "Sure. I'm glad that someone in this department cares about what the employees think."

In this example the "client" is clearly exasperated and is considering rather drastic action. Reflecting strong feelings and offering to listen is the first step in what may become a counseling interview.

Once you have initiated a counseling interview in either of the two ways described, it may proceed for just a few minutes or for more than an hour. You simply must follow the client's lead. You cannot counsel someone who is unwilling to open up and talk. But, given a responsive client, there is much that you can do to make the interview successful.

**Listen.** While it is essential that you listen carefully throughout the counseling interview, listening is particularly important during the first stage of the interview directed toward problem definition. Watch for strong feelings in facial expressions or tone of voice as well as the ideas which the feelings accompany. You will need to deal with the feelings *first*, before going into the actual ideas which the client is conveying.

**Focus and Probe.** There are a number of ways in which you can respond to what the client says, but each response should be aimed at keeping the channels of communication open. As you listen to the client, you will need to store points that you will turn to later by focusing on them and probing for more detail. In the counseling interview you must pay special attention to how your responses affect the client and the communication flow. The following example will illustrate this point.

Consider yourself talking with a woman in her late twenties who is currently employed as an accountant. You are the manager of the department and during a visit to your office she says the following:

> "I've been in this office for three years now—and in the same department for two years—but I hardly know anybody in the department. I just can't seem to make friends. I just freeze up—I try to be nice to the clerical staff and the other accountants, but I feel all stiff and uncomfortable inside. And then I tell myself that I don't care. People aren't dependable. Everyone is out for himself. I don't want any friends—and sometimes I think I really mean that."

This employee is obviously feeling a lot of frustration and is very openly asking for help. Your role as a counselor is to respond to what she has said and enter into a counseling interview. See the five responses following that you could give. They are illustrations of five different types of responses. Read them carefully and choose the ones that you think are appropriate.

1. "Well, I'll tell you what I can do. I can arrange for you to join a special interest group in the office. I have given that advice to quite a few people who have difficulty in making friends. Most start out attending discussion programs, coffee hours, lectures, or some other program. This gives them something to get interested in and an opportunity to make friends slowly and at their own pace."

2. "Could you tell me a little more about how you go about trying to make friends so we could get a clearer idea of what is involved?"

3. "It's gone on so long it almost has you convinced—is that what you mean?"

4. "Maybe your not wanting friends is just to protect you from something else."

5. "That's a pretty unhappy situation, to be without friends, and one that I would really work on. There are a number of things that you might do to learn how to make friends and the sooner you start, the better."

1. *Solution.* Now I want to examine each response in detail. The first is clearly a solution, and as such it is premature. The manager has reached into a drawer and pulled out a quick solution before the problem has been defined. This suggestion may indeed be appropriate and useful to the accountant, but the manager should not raise it until after the problem has been explored and defined.

A word of caution here: There are fundamental reasons why counselors give a quick solution to a client. Some do so in an attempt to reduce the discomfort that the problem causes either them or their client to feel. It's a relief to all concerned to have the problem solved quickly. In addition, when there is a clear difference in power or status between the counselor and the client, some counselors are prone to jump to a quick solution. People in positions of authority, such as managers, teachers, and parents, must be particularly mindful of suspending judgment and withholding solutions until they have allowed the client to define the problem.

The counselor who gives a quick solution runs still another risk. The counseling interview ends ideally when the client produces the solution. Clients are generally more committed to solutions they work out themselves, and they are more likely to recognize their own responsibility in making the solution work. If your suggestion to the client is not effective, you may find yourself bearing the blame for its failure.

2. *Question.* The next response in the illustration is a very useful open-ended question that asks the client to add some information which may reveal a potential cause of her frustration. It focuses on one particular element of what she has expressed—how she tries to make friends—and then probes for more detail.

3. *Show understanding.* In this response, the counselor shows some understanding of the predicament by reflecting the mixture of frustration and futility the client is expressing. By reflecting these feelings, the counselor is focusing on a specific element of the client's initial statement and is encouraging her to elaborate on her feelings.

4. *Interpretation.* This response is inappropriate. In making this comment, the counselor is assuming the role of amateur psychiatrist and is interpreting the client's behavior in terms of an underlying psychological cause. Such a response is not useful in a counseling interview for two reasons. First, a part-time counselor is very likely unqualified to make a psychological diagnosis, especially on such limited information. Second, such a response is very unlikely to be useful to the client. It may make her feel defensive. It may frighten her. It will almost certainly reduce the flow of communication between herself and the counselor.

5. *Evaluation.* In this response, the counselor is using personal values to judge the severity of the client's predicament. In the counselor's view, being without friends is an unhappy situation that needs urgent attention. Indeed, most people would agree. But the *timing* of such an evaluation is the important matter here. It has come much too early in the interview. The client may have many friends outside work. She may come to realize that the reason she has not become friends with her colleagues at work is that she finds little in common with them or dislikes her chosen line of work. While the counselor's intention in making this statement may be to motivate the client, it can backfire. As a counselor, you should make evaluative statements only when the client is weighing alternatives and needs your direction.

In focusing and probing in the counseling interview, you need to remain as neutral as possible as you seek to help the client define the problem. In each of the three inappropriate responses—solution, interpretation, and evaluation—the counselor was responding to personal values and needs as well as to the client's need for assistance. You have to work very hard as a counselor to ignore your own needs and values and focus on the need of the client to define the problem, consider alternatives, and develop a plan for change.

**Use.** The last step in the five-step sequence of initiate–listen–focus–probe–use is of particular importance in the counseling interview. The most effective counseling interview will not end until the client has set a plan of action and is clearly committed to that plan. As a counselor, you have the responsibility of helping the client use what has been discussed earlier in the interview to set plans and goals. Consequently, you need to direct the client's attention toward the future with comments such as the following:

> "I think we've reached a pretty clear understanding of what has been troubling you. What do you think you can do to change the situation?"
>
> or
>
> "You seem quite eager to work your way out of this dilemma. What steps are open to you?"

You may have an opportunity to give your views on the feasibility of various alternatives in this final stage of the interview. You may wish to evaluate the planning that the client is doing, or you may even offer your own solution. How directive you become depends largely on how much the client appears to be receptive to your ideas or whether the client even openly asks for them. I recommend that you follow the client's lead and, when offering a solution, put it in the form of a proposal for the client to consider. For example,

> "I've got an idea that I'd like to try out on you. Would it be possible for you to . . .?"
>
> or
>
> "As we talked this whole situation through, I've come up with an idea that I'd like you to think about. What do you think of the possibility of . . .?"

It is generally desirable to withhold your own views until after you have sought out the perceptions and proposals of the client. And when you make your proposals in the form of the examples given, you are giving the client a choice, not a guaranteed solution. This will ensure that the client accepts responsibility for the plans which are worked out in the counseling interview. On the other hand, if you give strong advice or promote a specific solution, you run the risk of accepting responsibility for the solution. If it fails, the client may blame you.

## MANAGING THE COUNSELING INTERVIEW

The counseling interview demands much of you as an interviewer. Although you have a set of objectives and a format, you do not enter the interview with content that you have worked out prior to the interview. Indeed, you may not even be aware that you have entered a counseling interview until you are in one. And yet, once you find yourself in a counseling interview, it is your responsibility to run it effectively. This will require you to draw heavily on the art of interviewing to manage the counseling interview.

Managing the interview involves two basic functions. The first is to draw out central themes and ideas from what you hear the client saying. This is similar to putting a jigsaw puzzle together. Many clients have not thought their situations through thoroughly, and so they give you a relatively disorganized combination of symptoms, perceptions, and proposals. Your challenge is to integrate what you hear and feed it back in a more organized way. This is hard work which takes a good deal of ability to think conceptually. But you have the advantage of hearing for the first time what has been whirling around in the client's mind for weeks or even months. Listen very carefully, focusing and probing with the techniques discussed earlier in the chapter. Then periodically summarize the emerging themes.

Your second function in managing counseling interviews is to keep clients moving through your format so that you can meet all four objectives in the interview. First, you need to keep clients from repeating themselves by drawing their attention to central themes which emerge in the interview. Second, you need to keep them moving from problem definition to problem solving and from problem solving to planning. Sometimes this may require a gentle nudge. You may have to turn their attention by asking future-oriented questions, such as

> "I think we both understand your predicament pretty well. Let's think now about what your options are."
>
> or
>
> "I think we have a good list of options. Which one appears most feasbile to you?"
>
> or
>
> "I agree that you do need to change jobs. I think it's important that you develop a plan of action to meet this goal. Let's see if we can work out a detailed strategy."

If you are able to manage the counseling interview in this way, both you and your client can succeed in meeting your respective needs. You will assist the client in meeting his or her need for help, and you will find yourself in the company of a less distressed companion.

# 5

# *Career Planning Interviewing*

We have entered an era in which many people are seeking *careers*, not "just a job." In this era of heightened career orientation, people have developed high expectations for personal growth and self-fulfillment in their work lives. Sometimes these expectations can be unrealistically high, especially among recent graduates with bachelors or masters degrees who enter an organization with the naïve view that they can rise in their careers in a very short period of time. These expectations for a work life that is not only materially rewarding, but also personally fulfilling, whether realistic or not, have spawned a desire among employees to manage their own careers. They want to know where they are headed in their work lives and how each job they take fits into an overall plan of career development. They are particularly interested in learning as much as possible from each job and each employer as they strive to grow in their work. To put it bluntly, many employees seem today to be at least as interested in what their employer can do for them as they are in what they can do for their employer.

Of course, self-interest has always been common among employees. Fundamentally, we all work for ourselves first, and, since our performance usually contributes to the goals of our employer, both parties benefit. It does appear, however, that some of the unwritten rules governing employee behavior have changed during this era of heightened career orientation. Employees appear less strongly committed to their employer. They are less willing to transfer. They change jobs and employers more often than in the past. Some of you may remember when turnover was considered a sign of instability in people, and having changed jobs more than two or three times in a five-year period was viewed negatively. Today, this level of turnover is likely to be viewed as a positive sign of upward mobility and career development!

As a manager responsible for the job performance of your employees, you can expect to be affected by this strong desire among employees to plan and develop their own careers. You will probably be influenced from two directions. New employees will look to you for information and guidance in developing their own careers. In addition, your boss or the personnel department of your company may expect you to take a more active role in developing the careers of the employees who report to you. How can you respond effectively to these added responsibilities of career development?

The answer to this question is for you to *enter into* the career planning which your employees are already doing. Your task is to help them do a better job of developing their own careers by giving them information and guidance. It is important for you to remember that, in career development, what is good for your employees is generally also good for you and your company. Employees who progress from job to job, expanding their potential to perform and increasing their satisfaction with their work, will become more valuable to their organization in the process *if they remain with that organization.* This leads us to your role as a manager in career planning. If you can help employees develop so that they perform at the top of their potential, and if you can also retain them in the organization, both the employees and your company benefit. Career planning is a means of ensuring that this development of employees occurs for the benefit of both the employee and the employer.

## DEFINITION OF CAREER PLANNING

Let's take a closer look at career planning. A definition of career planning must begin with a definition of career. Hall[1] defines career as "the individually perceived sequence of attitudes and behaviors associated with work-related experiences and activities over the span of a person's life." There are several conclusions that we can draw from this definition.

First, career is a very personal phenomenon. "Individually perceived" implies that each of us defines his or her own career in his or her own terms. What may appear to someone else to be a very unsuccessful or dissatisfying career may be very satisfying to the individual. Second, career is a lifelong sequence or process which develops and unfolds over time. This means that employees of any age and tenure are likely to be concerned with their careers. Third, the term "career" applies primarily to employees' work lives. While personal matters with a spouse or family may influence career planning, the planning which is done deals primarily with work. Finally, the phrase "attitudes and behaviors" indicates that careers encompass not only what people *do*, such as performing, earning money, or choosing between jobs, but also how they *feel* about what they do (satisfied, bored, frustrated, motivated). Often their feelings about their work can be more important to their career planning than what they are actually doing.

Career planning is the process through which one charts, monitors, evaluates, and adjusts one's own career. In a career planning interview, a second party (supervisor, manager, fellow employee, spouse, personnel specialist) assists someone in this process. To clarify the role of the second party who assists someone in career planning, let's return to our definition of career. What must you be aware of as a career planning interviewer?

## THE MANAGER'S ROLE IN CAREER PLANNING

First, as a manager or supervisor, you do career planning *with* someone, not *for* someone. Consequently, the responsibility for career planning is shared by you and the employee. Second, career planning requires you to get *inside the head* of the other person to learn about perceptions and plans regarding his or her own career. This requires that you collect a good deal of information. Finally, career planning is a dynamic process influenced by new information relating to the employee's work life. Since a career is a lifelong process, it is constantly open to evaluation and change. Your role in career planning therefore involves providing work-related information which contributes to the planning process of your employees.

I do not mean to suggest that most people plan their careers and then watch them unfold in a logical and predictable way. For many of us, quite the reverse is true. If we try to trace a logical pattern along the line our career has taken to date, we might be baffled by the sharp twists and turns which occurred. Why did the person who began college as a physics major opt for an MBA and become president of a land development company? Through what tangled trail did a company representative who visited 160 company locations per year wind up at the corporate headquarters of another company as manager of compensation?

As we look back, we see ourselves constantly evaluating and reevaluating our career choices as we received and reacted to new information. Remember that how we *feel* about work-related experiences and activities is an important element of our careers. We receive new information every day that affects our feelings about our work lives. The latest inflation figures suggest to us that we need a job in which we can earn more money. Being passed over for promotion suggests that we're going nowhere in this company. Finishing a project ahead of schedule and receiving recognition from the department head greatly increases commitment to the job and employer.

We are all in a constant state of absorbing new information and reevaluating our careers. Implicitly or explicitly, we are all in a continuing process of planning our own careers. What does this mean to you as a manager or supervisor who conducts career planning interviews? One of your main responsibilities as a manager or supervisor is to help employees perform as well as they are capable of performing and to retain those employees for as long as they perform well. To do so, you must enter into the career planning process in which your employees are constantly engaged. You need to make this a joint effort while each employee is a member of your organization. You have valuable information which your employees need to plan their careers more effectively. They, in turn, have a wealth of information which you must tap to help them plan their careers in a more informed way. The purpose of this chapter is to help you learn to enter and contribute to the career planning process of your employees in a useful way.

## OBJECTIVES

There are four major objectives of a career planning interview. They are

1. Identify satisfactions and dissatisfactions with the current job, career, and employer.
2. Identify employee work needs and goals.
3. Inform the employee of promotion opportunities and available career paths.
4. Formulate a career development plan.

Notice that as the interviewer, you are assuming three distinct roles in the career planning interview. The first two objectives require you to collect information from the employee. The third objective requires you to provide information to the employee. Hence, you must assume the quite different roles of information collector and information giver. Finally, you assume a third role of counselor as you and your employee work together to consider alternatives and make decisions to formulate a career development plan. Assuming three distinct roles to meet four objectives will certainly keep you on your toes in a career planning interview. This degree of complexity requires that you become quite familiar with the objectives you have to address *before* you enter the interview. Let's look at these four objectives in more detail.

**Objective 1: Identify satisfactions and dissatisfactions with the current job, career, and employer.**   It is in pursuit of the first objective that you must get inside your employees' heads and investigate their feelings about their work lives. What characteristics of the work and organization does the employee find particularly satisfying or dissatisfying? What opportunities do the job and the organization offer for advancement and future work satisfaction? You will need to give special attention to

nature of the work performed

what the employee likes and dislikes about the work

employee's perception of available opportunities for promotion inside and outside the organization

employee's satisfaction with advancement to date in his or her career and in the organization.

In this portion of the interview, you need to probe employees' perceptions and feelings about not only their work but also the opportunities the organization offers for them to advance their careers.

**Objective 2: Identify employee work needs and goals.**   The second objective requires you to identify what employees want from their work and how they plan to attain what they want. Of course, every employee will be pursuing somewhat different goals at work, but there are significant similarities among the work needs and goals of employees who are in the same stage of development in their careers.[2] Five *career development stages* are summarized now. However, these stages are not intended as a rigid formula; that is, not everyone in a given stage will have the same needs and goals. I have included a description of the five stages for you to use as general guides. Knowledge of the stages will help you focus more clearly on the issues which are of particular importance to each individual employee and tailor your interview more to the needs of that employee.

1. *Exploration stage.* This is an initial trial period in which individuals discover and experiment with various types of work. Because of limited prior work experience, expectations may be often unrealistically high among employees in this stage. They consider as very important opportunities to advance, to use their unique skills and educational background, to be recognized for their achievements, to be challenged at work, and to be paid well. Many face early disappointment, and change jobs and employers frequently in search of the work life that meets their high expectations.

2. *Establishment stage.* Having found a suitable kind of work, employees next turn their attention toward establishing and stabilizing their work lives. Safety and security emerge as important needs as employees strive to settle down and earn recognition and status in their chosen career through performance.

3. *Advancement stage.* Once employees feel that they have found their niche in the world of work and have attained sufficient levels of success to feel secure, the desire to create, develop, and advance at work becomes paramount. It is in this stage that we truly become masters of our trade and ideally develop as far as our intelligence, knowledge, and skills will allow.

4. *Maintenance stage.* This stage spans the greatest portion of our work life from age forty to age sixty-five. Much has been written about the beginning of this career stage, marked by the entry into the second half of one's life. Terms like "midlife crisis," "midcareer crisis," and "middle-aged" abound. About the only valid conclusion concerning this career stage is that it produces tremendously different effects on different people. Some shift into high gear and continue to develop and perform well and reach new heights in their work lives.

Others feel that life has passed them by and embark on twenty-five years of lower work goals and performance, which amounts to stagnation and decline in their work lives. Some observers of careers have characterized these people as acting for twenty years as though they were six months from retirement.

A third group of employees in this career stage have reached their level of competence and maintain that level of performance for another twenty years until retirement. They are the employees who are no longer on the "fast track" of advancement but can be the backbone of the organization: good, steady, reliable employees. While they look over their shoulders occasionally and see a world of younger people gaining on them, they continue to perform well in areas of work they have mastered.

Finally, there is still another group that enters the maintenance stage but does not remain there long. The maintenance stage does involve a good deal of soul searching, as employees realistically assess their own capabilities, their career choices, and their satisfaction with their work lives. Growing numbers of working people are beginning new careers at midlife and are beginning again at the exploration or establishment stage of career development. As the rate of change of the work world continues to increase, technological advances and information booms will force more people either to change careers at least once in their lifetimes or to struggle to keep up to date in their first careers.

5. *Retirement stage.* The final career stage is one of decline and retirement. At age sixty or later we end our work lives and move into a world of leisure and free time. This is a period of adjustment in which one's energy and goals, albeit declining, must be rechanneled if one is to go on living well and feeling satisfied with life.

**Objective 3: Inform the employee of promotion opportunities and available career paths.**   Your third objective in the career planning interview is to tell employees about what is possible within the organization. Focus the discussion on each available career path, a series of jobs through which employees can progress in their careers in the organization. For a clerical employee, a typical career path is receptionist → clerk typist → secretary → administrative assistant → supervisor. A business school graduate employed in the marketing department of a large consumer products company might consider the following career path: assistant product manager → product manager → brand manager → group manager. An accountant in a financial controls department of a medium-sized company might aspire to a career path such as accountant → intermediate accountant → senior accountant → supervisor → department manager → controller → financial vice president. You will need to do some research in your own department and company to identify potential career paths for your employees.

In many organizations, employees do not have a very clear understanding of career development opportunities. This is due primarily to lack of information. As I have already said, they need to know the jobs they can strive for to develop in their careers inside the company. To obtain this information, you will need to look at promotional opportunities not only inside your own department but also throughout the entire company.

But this is just the beginning. Employees must also know how to change their own knowledge and skills so they can prepare themselves to perform successfully in the next job in their career paths. Any planning process requires three basic pieces of information: (1) where we are now, (2) where we want to be in the future, and (3) how we get from here to there. Let's translate these fundamental steps into the context of career planning:

1. What is my current job?
2. To what job do I aspire?
3. In what ways do I have to develop as an employee to move from my current job to the next job?

In my years of university teaching and management consulting, I have seen distressingly few organizations in which there is sufficient information available to employees to answer these three deceptively simple questions. Job descriptions are frequently too general to provide sufficiently detailed information to answer questions 1 and 2 for career planning. Lists of training and development courses are potentially useful in identifying the methods of employee development, but they are most useful only after question 3 has been answered in terms of what the employee must learn to advance to the next job.

1. *Work performance guides.* To know if they can progress into another job, employees need to know what they must actually *do* on that job, what *knowledge* they need, and what *skills* they must use. This information can be summarized in a "work

performance guide," a very comprehensive job description that I have found to be very useful in career development. I recommend it to you as a basis for defining the jobs in your employees' career paths. Let's take a close look at what is contained in a work performance guide diagrammed in Figure 5.1.

2. *Performance targets.* The performance targets specify the job functions for which the employee is responsible. These targets can be broken down into four categories:

*Technical*—All jobs require that the employee perform a number of technical functions on data or things.

*Relational*—All jobs require that employees deal with others in simple or complex ways.

*Administrative*—All jobs require enforcing or following basic company policies and procedures during the course of the work.

*Innovative*—All jobs require employees to react to the unexpected and develop new ways of doing the work.

### FIGURE 5.1
### Work Performance Guide

```
        PERFORMANCE
        REQUIREMENTS


    KNOWLEDGE                    SKILL

    "Must Know"              "Must Be Able to Do"

  1. Technical               1. Technical
  2. Relational              2. Relational
  3. Administrative          3. Administrative
  4. Innovative              4. Innovative


        PERFORMANCE
        TARGETS

        "Make Happen"

      1. Technical
      2. Relational
      3. Administrative
      4. Innovative
```

The performance targets in these four basic areas clearly identify what an employee must get done on the job. They provide basic information to the process of career planning. Employees looking at a work performance guide for their current job can answer the question, "What am I capable of delivering to this organization? What performance targets can I meet?" Similarly, employees can look at a job to which they aspire and identify in detail what they must be able to do to move into that job. Table 5.1 provides a good illustration of performance targets.

**TABLE 5.1**
**Work Performance Guide**

---

Financial Controls    Treasury Department
Job:   Assistant Treasurer

---

Summary of Job Responsibilities

The Assistant Treasurer is primarily responsible for monitoring and maintaining the functions of cash receipts, cash disbursements, payroll, and cash management. He monitors these functions through supervising a banking supervisor and two financial analysts. He also periodically reviews a number of worksheets of the clerical staff and directs the staffing and cross-training of clerical personnel. Finally, he serves as a liaison with other departments in Financial Controls, Company operating departments, and Corporate Accounting, Treasury, and Legal departments.

Performance Targets, Technical

1. *Cash Disbursements.* Monitor the flow of cash disbursements with a regular review, sign checks over $10,000, and periodically review checks of under $10,000. Review and investigate related specific or general procedural problems when they arise and take appropriate action such as (a) make adjustments to respond to fluctuations in the computer schedule and heavy invoice load and (b) as required, make decisions to expedite or postpone certain disbursements.

2. *Cash Receipts.* Monitor the flow of cash receipts to ensure that all receipts have been properly recorded and accounted for by (a) reviewing and approving Daily Statements of Cash Receipts and (b) reviewing monthly reconciliation of cash receipts vouchers to the general ledger.

3. *Cash Management.* Monitor cash management function by (a) reviewing the Daily Wire Transfer Worksheet, (b) reviewing weekly the cash control worksheet, (c) reviewing monthly and weekly cash forecasts, (d) reviewing

# TABLE 5.1 (cont.)

monthly bank analysis statements, (e) reviewing monthly reconciliation of cash control to the general ledger, and (f) initiating lock box studies in accordance with standard policies and procedures.

4. *Payroll.* Monitor the payroll function to ensure that all employees are paid accurately and timely and that earnings records are maintained in accordance with Employee Relations, Tax, and Operating departmental requirements by (a) reviewing with the banking supervisor that all schedules have been met and (b) reviewing with the banking supervisor and approving vouchers, deduction registers, tax reports, and personnel reports.

Performance Targets, Relational

1. Direct cross-training of Treasury personnel to ensure that each job has a backup by (a) selecting employees to be trained and (b) setting the parameters (content and duration) of the training.

2. Make recommendations to the Treasurer for staffing requirements (RFPs) by reviewing functions, work load, and capability of available personnel.

3. Supervise, direct, and evaluate the work of a banking supervisor and two financial analysts.

4. Through personal contact and written communications, coordinate the flow of required information and reports to and from other Financial Controls departments, all other Company departments, Corporate Treasury, Corporate Legal, and Corporate Financial Controls.

5. Through personal contact and correspondence with various banking reps, monitor the appropriate relationships that the Company has with those banks.

Performance Targets, Administrative

1. Ensure that standard policies, procedures, and internal controls are complied with by (a) informing staff of the policies, procedures, and controls and (b) periodically reviewing checkpoints.

2. Periodically review and revise departmental policies, procedures, and internal controls and, when applicable, recommend changes in Company policies and procedures.

3. Make recommendations to the Treasurer re space, equipment, and systems needs.

Performance Targets, Innovative

1. Keep informed of developments in cash management, accounts payable, accounts receivable, and payroll techniques and principles and,

TABLE 5.1 (cont.)

when appropriate, incorporate them into our cash management and payroll systems.

2. Be informed of new techniques and principles in personnel development, supervision, and work and organizational design and recommend appropriate revisions.

3. Develop new policies and procedures and related forms, where needed and practicable.

4. Recognize those situations that involve Treasury, for example, information of a large product purchase or sale, new project, venture or acquisition, and act accordingly.

Knowledge, Technical

Technical knowledge listed applies to the following four areas: (a) cash disbursements, (b) cash receipts, (c) cash management, and (d) payroll.

1. Knowledge of each specific function.

2. Knowledge of Corporate and Company policies and procedures re each function.

3. Knowledge of related Company internal controls.

4. General working knowledge of accounting, finance, banking, computer systems, and company operations.

Knowledge, Relational

1. Knowledge of departmental work flow and capabilities of available staff.

2. Knowledge of training methods.

3. Knowledge of supervisory procedures.

4. Knowledge of needs of other departments for Treasury information and Treasury's needs for information from other departments.

5. Knowledge of organizational structure and who's who within the Company, the Corporate Office, and banks we deal with.

6. Knowledge of company policies and procedures regarding personnel.

Knowledge, Administrative

1. Knowledge of Company and Corporate policies and procedures and internal controls.

2. Knowledge of needs of the department for efficient operations.

## TABLE 5.1 (cont.)

Knowledge, Innovative

1. Knowledge of sources of information (trade publications, general business magazines, seminars, personal contact) re cash management, payroll, personnel development, and work and staff supervision.
2. Comprehensive understanding of departmental functions and the policies and procedures affecting them.

Skills, Technical

1. Observational skills.
2. Skill in defining and resolving problems.
3. Diagnostic and analytical skills to find causes of technical problems.

Skills, Relational

1. Supervisory skills.
2. Skills in written and verbal communication.
3. Training skill.
4. Skill to form and maintain good working relationships with staff and also with others not reporting to the Assistant Treasurer.
5. Ability to plan, set priorities, schedule work, and utilize workforce effectively.

Skills, Administrative

1. Ability to analyze, interpret, communicate, and implement standard policies and procedures and internal controls.
2. Ability to diagnose departmental needs for increased efficiency.

Skills, Innovative

1. Ability to recognize need for change.
2. Ability to present new ideas and procedures in a simple and practical way.

3. *Performance requirements.* Now let's move upward in Figure 5.1. What does it take to meet the performance targets? What is required of the employee? Knowledge and skill combine to produce performance. Both are essential. Consequently, the performance requirements are divided into two basic components:

*Knowledge*—What the employee must know to achieve the permance targets.

*Skill*—What the employee must be able to do to achieve the performance targets.

Each of these two performance requirements is divided into the same four categories that apply to performance targets: *technical, relational, administrative,* and *innovative.*

The example in Table 5.1 provides specific examples of knowledge and skill required to achieve performance targets. Notice that, while new recruits can be expected to bring some basic knowledge to the job from their educational background, much of the knowledge must be learned *after employment begins.* If you expect employees to perform their own jobs well or move to other jobs in the organization, you must give them opportunities to increase their knowledge and skill through your company's programs of employee development and career planning.

**Objective 4: Formulate a career development plan.**   In the fourth objective of the career planning interview, you need to address the last question in any planning process: "How do I get from here to there?" In the previous objectives, you and the employee have established what the employee wants and what potential jobs and career paths the organization can offer. In this final objective, you must identify the opportunities for employee development that will bridge the gap between where the employee is now and where he or she would like to be.

While each individual employee's career development plan is unique, some generalizations can be made about the kind of planning which is appropriate for employees at various stages of their careers. I have adapted the following suggestions from an excellent synthesis done by Hall.[3] They are based on the career stages discussed earlier in this chapter.

1. *Exploration stage.* Since employees in this stage of career development are just beginning to discover their likes and dislikes in the work world, they have strong needs for new information and a variety of job activities. Realistic, well-integrated orientation programs are essential for employees in the exploration stage. These programs enable new employees to learn what is expected

of them in their new jobs and therefore tend to eliminate that uneasy initial period in which employees sometimes grope around and learn their job responsibilities largely through trial and error.

Career planning in this stage often involves exposing employees to possibilities and choices. You can tell new employees about the range of job opportunities within a given department or organization, and together you and your employees can set out a plan to expose them to various job activities within the department or organization. You may decide to give either varied or special assignments to some employees or to rotate others from one job to another during the exploration stage. You may also wish to assemble detailed information on the nature of a number of jobs open to new employees, such as that found in work performance guides, as a basis for the process of career planning.

2. *Establishment stage.* After a period of exploration, new employees choose and commit themselves to a field of work and then begin to establish themselves in their chosen line of work. This begins a new stage of determining how well they can perform. In this stage of career development, most employees begin to discover the limits of the knowledge and skill they bring to the organization. Several questions arise. "What is easy or difficult for me? What do I like and dislike about this work? Have I made the right choice? How well do I really perform? Does anyone besides me recognize how well I am doing? Who is my competition for advancement? What new knowledge and skills do I have to learn to become a better performer?"

During career planning interviews with employees in the establishment stage, you may need to deal with some pretty fundamental feelings which employees develop toward their work — both positive and negative. You may have to draw heavily on your counseling skills (see Chapter 4) to help employees deal effectively with these feelings. Disillusionment, disappointment, and self-doubt may arise. You may have to help employees address rivalry and competition. Employees may need help in recognizing that they do have gaps of knowledge and skill.

Once you and the employee have dealt effectively with these feelings, the two of you can begin making career development plans. In brief, these plans should strengthen or test an employee's potential to perform. You may select additional challenging job assignments. Additional coursework in a specialty area may be needed. Employees may desire skill training to help them perform a specific job function more effectively.

3. *Advancement stage.* This stage of career development is a natural extension of the establishment stage. Once employees have settled into their field of work, they strive to progress as far as their talents and intentions will allow. Employees in the advancement stage need a good deal of feedback about their performance and appropriate support. As they become more competent in their work, they prefer greater autonomy to be creative and innovative. Since advancement is often accompanied by increased responsibility and demands for employees' attention and time, questions may arise regarding the relative priorities of work and family.

Designing a career development plan with employees in the advancement stage requires you to turn your attention to their talents and priorities. What special capabilities do the employees offer the organization? How far do they want to progress? What new knowledge and skill must they develop to reach their goals? When considering an employee's potential for advancement, you will have to look at the gaps between what the employee is presently doing and the performance requirements of the desired job. Organizations abound with good technicians and professionals who were promoted into managerial jobs *that they were not qualified to perform.* Successful promotion requires careful study of the work performance guides for the current and desired jobs, identification of the knowledge and skills needed for the step up, and a plan on how to fill those gaps. Finally, you must resist the temptation to discourage the advancement of a particularly competent employee reporting to you. Even though you may sometimes lose your best employee to promotion, you will generally serve your needs and the needs of the organization and the employee best by encouraging each employee to advance as far as possible.

4. *Maintenance stage.* This is the stage in which employees spend the bulk of their careers, and it is the stage that presents the greatest challenge to you in the career planning interview.

Employees in the maintenance stage may experience a myriad of challenges, stresses, and crises. Some employees will adjust to changes in themselves, their field of work, and their organizations better than others, but all need some support if they are to continue to perform effectively and gain satisfaction in their work lives.

Career planning in the maintenance stage must be very carefully attuned to the needs of the individual employee. You will have to help each employee make plans that suit his or her own career aspirations. Some may require updating in their chosen field through individual study or through seminars and conferences. Others who wish to assume the role of mentor may need to learn not only what to do on the job but how to coach and train younger employees. Finally, to keep them feeling challenged and to use their broad understanding of their field of work and their employer's business, still other employees in the maintenance stage may choose transfers to related jobs requiring new knowledge and skills.

5. *Retirement Stage.* Career planning with employees in the retirement stage is essentially a process of gradually redirecting their focus from work to nonwork. This is the area of career planning which has received the least attention from organizations in general and potential career planners in particular. Planning for retirement should ideally begin years, rather than months, before the actual retirement date.

Employees approaching retirement face the dual challenge of withdrawing psychologically from their work and increasing their involvement and commitment in the aspects of their lives not associated with work. The need to leave a legacy is strong, especially among employees who have led very involving and successful work lives. And many employees have much to offer the organization during preretirement. A crucial element of career planning in the retirement stage is for you to encourage and allow retiring employees to contribute what they can. You may want many to assume the role of resident expert, teacher of new employees, consultant, or reliable source of historical information, as they mold those who will take their place in the organization. With others you may simply make it clear that you do appreciate their work and that they will be missed. Whether employees approaching retirement feel passed by and useless or essential in preparing the organization for their absence depends largely on how you treat them during this crucial career stage.

## PLANNING THE CAREER PLANNING INTERVIEW

### APPROACH

As I have already said, the career planning interview is the most complex interview covered in this book, and as such it certainly requires a clear plan and structure. As always, I recommend a semistructured approach to meet the interview's objectives, but with the flexibility to allow the interviewer to respond and react to each individual employee.

Since the career planning interview begins with information collecting, it is necessary that as interviewers, you set out clearly the kind of information you need to collect during the interview. A similar plan is required in the information-giving portion of the interview; you will need to be familiar with the career development opportunities available in your organization which apply to the specific employee you are interviewing. Finally, since the career planning interview ends with action planning, I recommend that you conduct the final stage of the interview with an approach of mutual goal setting.

### BEFORE THE INTERVIEW

**Information collecting.**   There is a great deal you need to learn about the employee during the interview. There is, however, much you must know about the employee before you enter the interview, and this will usually necessitate some prior research into several of the following areas:

1. *Employment history.* What jobs has the employee held inside and outside your organization? What are the career relationships among those jobs (a logical progression or not)? What functions has the employee performed and what knowledge and skill does he or she offer? What is the employee's current job and what is the work performance guide for that job?

2. *Career stage.* In which stage of career development does the employee appear to be? Is the employee still exploring? Has the employee been established for ten years? How many years is the employee from retirement? Your hunch about the employee's current career stage will help you interpret what the employee says in the interview especially concerning work satisfactions, needs, and goals.

3. *Performance appraisals.* What has been this employee's level and consistency of performance since joining your organization? A review of the employee's performance appraisal file can give you some fruitful clues to pursue in the interview. Has the employee performed very well at times, but with intermittent slumps? Has the employee consistently done just what was expected, but nothing more? You may wish to speak with the employee's previous supervisors to gain additional insight. Be careful, however, not to form firm conclusions on the basis of this review. There are many explanations of why employees perform as they do, and the most valid ones often come directly from the employees themselves. This review is not to form conclusions but, rather, to raise questions you will pursue in the interview.

4. *Employee development.* Finally, review what the employee has done to develop in his or her career. Has the employee taken every employee development course available? Has the employee applied for other jobs within the company? How often has the employee been passed over for promotion? Why? This information will give you an idea of how career oriented the employee is. Some constantly seek out new developmental opportunities; others put in their eight hours and develop and experience their personal satisfaction in their nonwork lives. These

clues about an employee's degree of career orientation will help you tailor the interview more toward that individual employee's needs.

**Information giving.**  This section boils down simply to your description of the career development opportunities the company offers. This information includes the types of jobs available and the knowledge and skill required for each job, as well as employee development opportunities the company provides or supports. Prior to the interview, you must arm yourself with all the information you may need to counsel employees on how they can progress in their careers. This is a very critical step. Many companies do not make employees aware of the wealth of career development opportunities they offer. As a career planning interviewer, you must have this information. But remember that you are making employees aware of what is *possible.* Do not make any promises or commitments unless you have the authority to deliver.

## FORMAT

Given a complex set of objectives and a semistructured approach, the career planning interview needs a format. This one is recommended.

1. *Explain the purpose of the interview.* As with other interviews with your own employees (e.g., performance appraisal), you should schedule a career planning interview ahead of time and ask the employee to come prepared. Begin the interview by stating its purpose and setting an agenda such as "I'd like to begin by getting your views and your feelings about your current job and your work plans in the future. Then I'll fill you in on the opportunities the company has available for employee and career development. Finally, we'll work together to plot out a plan for your own career development and decide what we need to do to set the plan in action." It's important for you to set out clearly the three portions of the interview: information collecting, information giving, and mutual planning.

2. *Ask open-ended questions regarding satisfactions and goals.* Here you need to get the employee talking about how he or she feels about the job, the level of his or her performance, and the direction of his or her career. Be supportive during this portion of the interview and draw out themes in the employee's comments.

3. *Describe what is possible.* Now you need to add your information. Tailor your presentation to the employee's interests and needs (you would not be likely to explain the company's new management trainee program to a sixty-two year old employee making plans for retirement). It is important here that you not propose specific steps or give advice. Instead, offer alternatives from which employees may select what fits their needs.

4. *Discuss and set goals for development.* This is the portion of the interview in which employees make their choices and begin to plan. If a specific job is desired, what knowledge and skill does the employee lack? What training is available to increase those areas of knowledge and skill? What work experience is necessary to fill the gaps? Here your focus is on *ends*, the goals the employees set, and the *means*, intervening steps and actions necessary to meet those goals.

5. *Propose follow-up.* End the career planning interview with a schedule for monitoring employee progress toward the goals. This is a crucial step if career planning is to become a genuine occurrence in a company rather than just an impressive but hollow phrase. Many companies engage in career planning, but relatively few actually plan and *develop* careers. Since career development is a long-term activity, it requires careful monitoring and follow-up.

## CONDUCTING THE CAREER PLANNING INTERVIEW

With a set of objectives and a format forming the skeleton of the interview, let's discuss how you can proceed with conducting the career planning interview. I advise you to rely on my standard sequence of initiate–listen–focus–probe–use in conducting the interview. In particular, this sequence will apply to the information-gathering and goal-setting stages of the interview.

**Initiate.**    After you have restated the purpose of the interview and set the agenda, you want to enter stage 2 of the format by getting the employee talking about his or her current job and career. Begin with questions such as

> "Now that you have been with us for nearly a year as a process engineer, what are your feelings about the job?"
>
> or
>
> "What aspects of your job do you find the most satisfying?"

Similarly in stage 4, where you begin to set goals for career development, open-ended questions like the following are useful:

> "Well, then, if you have no additional questions about the options open to you at this time, I'd like to turn our attention to some planning for the future. What career goal would you like to pursue?"
>
> or
>
> "I feel our discussion has been very fruitful so far. Let's start thinking about what happens next. What steps do you think would help you develop best in your career with us?"

**Listen.**    Next, you must listen for points to pursue. Look for underlying themes in the employee's comments. His or her long-term interest is toward management. He or she wants to remain a specialist. He or she seems uncertain and is leaning toward further exploration. Listen for any feelings, such as dissatisfaction, frustration, excitement, or impatience. These reflect needs and career stages.

**Focus and Probe.**    As themes or issues arise in the interview that you wish to pursue in more detail, focus on them and then probe. Remember to use the nondirective techniques of reflecting a feeling or an idea and then ask a direct question to gather more information. For example,

> "You sound a bit frustrated. Is there something about the work that is bothering you?"

or

"I gather that you really enjoy the challenge in that project. Would you like more challenge?"

or

"It seems to me from what you've said so far that seeing a product of your efforts on the job is pretty important to you. Is that right?"

**Use.** In the context of the career planning interview, this step becomes most prominent in stage 4 of the format—discussing and setting goals for development. It is important for you to avoid planning *for the employee.* Instead, ask what the employee wants to achieve and how he or she wants to proceed. Your role is to counsel and guide. In particular, help the employee to distinguish between *ends,* such as target jobs or long-term career goals, and *means* to these ends, such as home study, a training course, job rotation, or cross-training.

Your primary intention is to help employees to set a career development plan to match their work needs and career goals. As interviewer, you have the responsibility of seeing that the planning process takes place in a logical and orderly way. This occurs in stage 4 of the interview. In the first three stages, you have established two main points:

1. What the employee wants.
2. What the company can provide or support.

Your focus in stage 4 is on

3. How to bridge the gap between where the employee is now and where he or she wants to be.

The goals you and the employee set together will very likely fall into one or a combination of the following action plans:

1. *Change the employee*—Add knowledge, skill, or work experience through training on or off the job.
2. *Alter the job*—Change the nature of the work done by the employee by adding desired functions or eliminating undesired functions.
3. *Find a new job*—Transfer or promote an employee to meet career goals.
4. *Find a new employer*—Sometimes filling the gap between what an employee wants and what a company can provide can be done only

through the employee's resignation. This may occur because of unrealistically high employee expectations or the employee's inability to develop and perform in an acceptable way. It may also occur because the company simply cannot provide the employment opportunity the employee desires.

You will have been most effective as a career planning interviewer if you and the employee leave the interview with a clear understanding of the employee's career development goal, the steps necessary to meet that goal, and a schedule for monitoring and following up.

## CAREER PLANNING
## AND PERFORMANCE APPRAISAL

Throughout this book I have pointed out how various interviews are related to and sometimes complement one another. This is particularly true for the performance appraisal and career planning interviews. Indeed, one of the objectives of the performance appraisal interview listed in Chapter 3 is "to promote career development by discussing long-range plans for development and promotion." The systematic discussion in performance appraisal interviews of how well employees perform their work and how they can improve certainly contributes to a climate of career development in an organization and also provides raw material about the level of performance an employee is capable of achieving.

While these two types of interviews complement one another, I strongly urge that *both* be conducted regularly in organizations committed to developing and retaining their employees. There are important differences between the two types of interviews. The career planning interview builds on the performance appraisal interview and takes planning for employee development a step farther. First, it provides information to employees about career development opportunities offered by the company that they otherwise might not learn about. (On August 12, 1980, *The Wall Street Journal* reported a Manpower Institute study indicating that, of 1.6 million employees eligible for tuition aid, only 4 percent of white-collar and 1 percent of blue-collar employees use it, the reason being lack of knowledge about the fringe benefit.) Second, the career planning interview focuses not only on employee performance (the prime emphasis of performance appraisal interviews) but also on employee needs, motivation, and intention. These are very important elements of the equation for matching employees with jobs. Third, career planning interviews take a longer look forward than the performance appraisal interview does in plotting the career prospects offered by the company. This longer-range planning would tend to lead to more highly integrated and career-oriented programs of employee development which would indicate to employees that remaining with one company is still a viable way to develop their careers.

## OUTPLACEMENT

One possible result of a career planning interview is the realization that the employee's career development is best served by leaving the company. This may occur because the employee cannot perform to the standards necessary to advance in the company. It may also occur because the kind of work to which the employee aspires is simply unavailable in the company. Especially in cases where the employee is terminated or resigns because of inadequate performance, an increasing number of companies are providing outplacement service to the employees.[4] This service consists essentially of career counseling and assistance in finding a new job. It is a logical extension of the career planning process in the company. While this service is expensive, it certainly promotes within the company a climate of commitment to employees and their career development, and I expect such outplacement service to continue in the future in major organizations.

## THE PROTEAN CAREER

I began this chapter by commenting on how the rules governing employee behavior have changed in the recent decade. In particular, employee turnover is more acceptable, and employees have become more intent on moving to the employer who will help them most in developing their own careers. Drawing on the Greek myth of Proteus, who was able to change his shape and size at will, Hall[5] has applied the term *protean career* to this emerging set of career-related values and behaviors. He defines the protean career as "a process which the person, not the organization, is managing."

Employees who aspire to the protean career, and their number is growing, want more control over their work lives. They want more freedom, more flexibility, and more options, and they are willing to change jobs and organizations frequently to obtain what they want. In the extreme, they are managing their own careers *in spite of their employer* rather than *in collaboration with their employer.* As a manager, your challenge is to enter into and contribute to the career planning process your employees are managing. If you can do so effectively, you and your organization will likely develop better employees and retain them longer. This will benefit both the employees and your organization.

# 6

# *Disciplinary Interviewing*

Almost all supervisors and managers will tell you that they dislike having to discipline their employees. The disciplinary interview is an uncomfortable situation for both parties. In these interviews, bosses often feel themselves slipping into the role of the punitive parent, and employees feel they are being treated as children. As a result, employees can become very defensive and argumentative, and bosses can become exceedingly frustrated. These strong negative emotions are certainly unpleasant for both parties and undermine the success of the interview. Indeed, a good deal of skill is required to conduct an effective disciplinary interview.

What is a disciplinary interview? It is a discussion between an employee and his or her immediate supervisor to correct the employee's failure to perform at an acceptable level. Usually it is triggered by a specific incident in which the employee's performance is unacceptable. Unacceptable performance may be a violation of company policy or professional standards (e.g., theft, frequent absenteeism, failure to attend a departmental meeting), or it may be failure to perform any assigned task well enough to meet the supervisor's standards. When an employee violates company

151

policy or professional standards, the supervisor may conduct a disciplinary interview after one such incident. For failure to perform assigned tasks, however, a disciplinary interview is usually appropriate after the employee has failed to perform up to standard a number of times.

Employee-made errors take two forms: those of commission and those of omission. In the case of *errors of commission*, the employee has performed a function or assignment but has failed to do it properly. For example, a programmer may write a subroutine that doesn't work, a secretary may send a letter containing two misspelled words, or a salesperson may reduce the price without proper authorization to meet a sales quota.

In the case of *errors of omission*, the employee has failed to do something that he or she was responsible for doing. Examples of errors of omission are a programmer who does not document the subroutine he or she has written, the secretary who fails to inform the boss when taking a day off work, or the salesperson who does not keep up to date on the technical innovations for the product he or she is selling.

## WHY DISCIPLINARY INTERVIEWS
## ARE NECESSARY

A crucial first step to changing employee performance is to understand the cause of the performance. There are, of course, a variety of reasons why employees fail to perform up to the standards of their supervisors or according to company policy, but they can be grouped into a manageable number of categories.

1. *Employee is not capable.* There are many instances in which an employee's lack of performance can be traced simply to his or her inability to do the job. The employee may be in the wrong job. The employee may not have the necessary knowledge and skill to perform up to standard. In these cases corrective action may involve training, redefinition of the current job, or even transfer to another job.

2. *Employee resists performing well.* In this category we find the so-called "problem employee" with a "poor attitude." These employees are capable of performing well, but their performance is inconsistent and unpredictable. They appear to lack the degree of commitment required to do their best at work. The root of their unacceptable performance is either the low priority which they attach to their work lives or a strong dissatisfaction with a major element of their current work situation—the work itself, the salary, the co-workers, the company, the boss, or the opportunities for promotion. Corrective action with those employees requires that the source of their dissatisfaction be uncovered and addressed.

3. *Employee doesn't know the rules.* A major and distressingly common cause of poor employee performance is lack of clear job definition and feedback from the supervisor. A remarkably large number of employees simply do not know what is expected of them on the job. In these cases a major portion of the responsibility for unacceptable performance rests squarely on the shoulders of the immediate supervisor. The source of the problem may be a lack of job descriptions, unclear instructions being given by the supervisor, an inadequate performance appraisal system, an absence of company operating procedures for various jobs, or supervisors who do not give feedback to their employees. Corrective action in these instances is twofold. First, jobs must be structured and defined in such a way that employees know what is expected of them. Second, supervisors must provide regular positive and negative feedback to employees regarding their performance so they can learn how to improve their work.

## OBJECTIVES

It is essential that, as interviewers, you have a clear idea of what you intend to achieve in the disciplinary interview. Knowing your objectives is particularly important in this interview because it is triggered by some sort of problem and almost invariably leads to emotional reactions from both parties. Unless you have clearly in mind what you want to achieve, you can easily be sidetracked or even lose control of the interview.

There are three basic objectives in the disciplinary interview. They are

1. *Define the situation*—Clearly describe the incident of unacceptable performance that has triggered the interview.
2. *Pinpoint the responsibility for failure*—Examine the causes of the unacceptable performance from both the interviewer's and the interviewee's point of view.
3. *Identify the corrective action*—Set out a specific plan of action to reduce or eliminate the unacceptable performance.

In the case of the disciplinary interview, these objectives also represent conditions for success. Each of the three is extremely crucial, and each must be met effectively before those following it can even be addressed. In short, you must achieve each objective well, and you must address all three of them in the sequence given.

**Define the situation.** In the first objective, you and your employee must clearly establish the reason for the interview, namely, the unacceptable performance. It is necessary that both parties give their perceptions of the incident that triggered the interview. Special attention should be given to

1. Exactly what the employee did that is viewed as unacceptable.
2. The severity of the employee's unacceptable performance.
3. What the employee was supposed to have done.
4. The circumstances surrounding the incident.

Here the policies and standards of the organization and the supervisor come into play. As the interviewer, you must consider how much human error is inevitable and how severe or chronic the unacceptable performance actually is.

**Pinpoint the responsibility for failure.** The second objective is to examine the factors and circumstances which contributed to the unacceptable performance. Which of the three general reasons why employees fail to perform (employee is not capable, employee resists performing well, or employee doesn't know the rules) seems to apply in this particular case? The views of both the supervisor and the employee must be brought out. A reminder: It is crucial that you keep your mind open to the possibility that you contributed to the problem either by not clearly defining the employee's job and your performance standards or by not giving the employee clear and consistent feedback.

**Identify the corrective action.**    Finally, in the third objective, you and your employee must turn toward the future. After you have identified the unacceptable performance and its cause, you must take whatever steps are necessary to eliminate or reduce the unacceptable performance. The interview cannot end successfully if you have not addressed this objective fully. It should end with a specific plan of action endorsed by you and, as often as possible, also by your employee.

## PLANNING THE DISCIPLINARY INTERVIEW

### APPROACH

The disciplinary interview should be approached with a clear plan and a well-defined format. The result will be a semistructured interview. The hallmark of the disciplinary interview is *direct and clear communication and mild confrontation.* By this I mean that you must be direct and clear in stating your views on what the employee has done poorly and why. Beating around the bush or being evasive will only confuse the employee. In addition, you must be prepared to confront the employee by pointing out inconsistencies in what he or she has said and done.

### BEFORE THE INTERVIEW

In planning a disciplinary interview, you must collect a good deal of information upon which you can draw in the interview. You must be prepared with facts that are properly documented. You must also do some research to try to understand the particular employee whom you are disciplining. This research will provide the background against which you can interpret what the employee has done before the interview and what he or she says during the interview. There are three major steps in this planning process.

**Step 1: Review and properly document employee performance.** This is a crucial first step. As the interviewer, you must collect all the facts concerning what the employee did or failed to do, and what the results of the unacceptable performance were. In most companies there will also be a set procedure for supervisors to follow in documenting the performance. Many company policies and union contracts require that first a verbal and then a written warning be given to the employee. These actions by the supervisor would generally precede a disciplinary interview. I suggest that before the interview you document in writing the actions of the employee and the results of those actions.

It is also essential that you examine the circumstances under which the unacceptable performance occurred. *How have you or the organization contributed to this failure?* Were you clear in your instructions to the employee? Are the job and this employee's specific responsibilities defined clearly? Is company policy clear on this violation? Have you, through inadequate feedback, allowed the employee to get away with this before? Be honest with yourself as you seek to uncover any way in which you must share responsibility for your employee's action.

**Step 2: Review performance appraisals for clues.** The next step is to review the employee's past performance either through formal performance appraisal files or your own recollection. Has the employee's performance been consistent or inconsistent? How well has the employee typically done in the past? Is this an unusual slump in an otherwise consistent and excellent record or is this one more incident in a long stream of unacceptable performance?

A particularly fruitful portion of the performance appraisal file is plans for employee development. Review these for several years to see if they have been acted on either by the employee or by the organization. Has the employee been turned down for a transfer or special training three years in succession? Did the employee perform poorly in a rotation program just before his or her recent promotion? Be on the lookout either for signs of the employee's inability to do the job or signs of frustration and anger in his or her work life. Why has this employee performed poorly?

**Step 3: Check your broad understanding of the employee.** Finally, reflect on your overall understanding of your employee. Why would the employee do such a thing? This behavior is unusual; what's changed? Although we may work with people forty hours a week, we really know little about them. Think back. What has happened on or off the job to frustrate, upset, or disillusion the employee? Form your hunches now and be prepared to examine them in the interview.

## FORMAT

As with other interviews covered in this book, I recommend a semistructured approach to the disciplinary interview. There are three objectives to be met and many questions to be answered in this interview, but the approach must be flexible enough to enable you to adjust the interview to the individual employee. There is, however, a basic format that forms the skeleton of the disciplinary interview. I recommend the following format.

1. *Set the ground rules.* It is important that, as the interviewer, you be clear in stating the purpose of your meeting with the employee. The need for such an interview should be no surprise to the employee if you have already given him or her verbal and written feedback regarding the unacceptable prformance. Therefore, you may summarize your intention in the interview by stating that you would like to discuss the incident in more detail and come up with a plan to prevent its recurrence. Emphasize also that you are very interested in the employee's point of view.

2. *Discuss the unacceptable performance.* It is preferable to begin by briefly summarizing the incident and then asking for the employee's perception of exactly what happened and why. In this section of the interview, it is necessary that you draw out details concerning what the employee did or failed to do, the circumstances surrounding the incident, and the results of the incident. After the employee has expressed his or her view, you present your perception of the incident. The main purpose in this section of the interview is to describe what happened, from the point of view of both the employee and the interviewer.

3. *Discuss the reasons for the unacceptable performance.* Here you are examining the factors that contributed to the employee's unacceptable performance. Be prepared to investigate each of the three reasons why employees fail to perform (employee is not capable, employee resists performing well, and employee doesn't know the rules) to ensure a thorough understanding of all potential causes.

4. *Make plans for change.* After a thorough diagnosis of the reasons for the unacceptable performance, the final step is to plan corrective action. Before the interview is closed, you and your employee should have a set of specific goals or assignments to be pursued by the employee with appropriate support from you or others in the company.

## CONDUCTING THE DISCIPLINARY INTERVIEW

The format, based on a set of objectives, forms the skeleton of the disciplinary interview. As with all other interviews in this book, the disciplinary interview comes to life through the skill and techniques you use in conducting it. The art of conducting the interview is particularly important in the disciplinary interview. You must be direct, clear, and firm. You must move through the entire interview format to cover all three objectives. You must deal on the spot with a variety of reactions from your employees;

they may become very emotional, deny apparent facts, or even lie.

Your main challenges in conducting the disciplinary interview are to draw out and examine what your employee has to say, to use mild confrontation to separate fact from fiction, and to make constructive use of the information you gain. To meet these challenges, I recommend that you rely on the familiar sequence of initiate–listen–focus–probe–use. More specifically, in the second and third sections of the format (discuss the unacceptable performance and discuss the reasons for the unacceptable performance), you will use the first four steps in the sequence to gather information. In the fourth section of the interview (make plans for change), you and the interviewee will focus on the last step in the sequence.

**Initiate.**   Begin the discussion of unacceptable performance with open-ended questions to encourage the employee to tell his or her perception of the incident. For example,

> "You know of my concern about the two clients who canceled their orders with us. In your view, what happened?"
>
> or
>
> "As you know, I have received three separate complaints in the last month that you violated safety standards. What is your perception of these three incidents?"

Later in the interview, when you are examining the reasons for the employee's performance, you will again use open-ended questions such as

> "Why did you decide to handle it the way you described?"
>
> or
>
> "What contributed to your decision to override company policy on that occasion?"

**Listen.**   As the employee responds to your open-ended questions, you should listen very carefully for points you wish to pursue. During the employee's description of what he or she did, listen for points that need elaboration or clarification. While the

employee explains his or her performance, listen for contradictions or points of contention. As a general rule, listen for questions that arise and must be examined further.

Remember that, during this portion of the interview, your
task is to collect information from the employee. Do so, silently.
You must resist the temptation to interrupt and voice your opinion. At this point, you need to keep the channels of communication wide open to learn as much as possible. If you hear something
that you disagree with or find confusing, store it in your memory
for additional examination later. If you feel you are being lied to,
avoid confronting the employee immediately. Give the employee
a few minutes to make his or her presentation as a whole and then
move in with your additional questioning. In short, while you are
listening, suspend judgment and avoid interrupting or delivering a
lecture.

**Focus and Probe.**  As always, this is where you do your real
work in the interview. Focusing on specific points and probing
them in more detail is particularly important in the disciplinary interview. You and your employee are at odds with one another.
You will hear things that you disagree with or oppose strongly. It
is your main task in the disciplinary interview to get these points
on the table and to deal with them in a direct and clear manner.

You will move through the initiate–listen–focus–probe sequence first as you examine the employee's perception of *what* occurred and then again as the employee explains *why* it occurred.
In each case, when you begin to focus and probe, start with issues
that are not highly contentious. Begin with issues that are least
likely to make the employee feel defensive. For example,

> "You mentioned that, by the time you realized that you had forgot-
> ten to notify the committee members of the meeting, it was too late
> to do anything. When did you realize that you had forgotten to
> notify them?"
>
>                         or
>
> "And you said that you felt the situation didn't warrant standard
> safety precautions. What factors did you consider in making that
> judgment?"

In these illustrations you are seeking more information so that you can understand more clearly what the employee did and why. It is crucial that you probe these areas in as neutral a fashion as possible, so that the employee does not feel attacked and, as a result, say little in response.

As you continue to focus and probe, you will need to work up to more contentious issues. These issues can take a variety of forms. You may find contradictions between what employees say and what they do. You may hear distortions of facts or outright lies. You may hear complaining and whining rather than valid reasons for inadequate performance. In these kinds of cases, you will have to confront employees with the discrepancy between what they say in the interview and the facts as you perceive them. Remember, though, your information may be wrong. Therefore, confront the employee with the discrepancy and ask for an explanation. Consider the following two examples:

A clerical employee in a bank has taken a parking pass from the manager's desk to cover a parking fee in a nearby lot. Bank policy states that these parking passes are available to customers only. The manager began the next day's work with a disciplinary interview. After hearing the employee's explanation of what occurred and why, the manager confronted the employee in the following way:

INTERVIEWER:  "You said earlier that you used the parking pass only because a loan officer gave you permission to use it. That simply doesn't fit with what I've learned about this incident. I saw you talking with three deposit clerks at the counter, and, when I talked to them later, each said you asked for a parking pass for your own use. Furthermore, I've checked my supply of passes, and one is missing. How do you explain the discrepancy between your explanation and what I have just said?"

The performance of a young person who has been in an entry-level job for six months has fallen off dramatically in the past two months. After commenting on the drop in performance on several occasions, and issuing a written warning, the manager has called the employee in for a disciplinary interview.

INTERVIEWER:   "So your main explanation for your drop in performance is that you are disappointed with the nature of the work. You feel that you have not been challenged enough on the job. Does that pretty well summarize what you said earlier?"

EMPLOYEE:   "Yes, I really feel frankly that I was promised a lot more than the company has delivered so far."

INTERVIEWER:   "To be equally frank with you, I'm having trouble accepting your explanation. On three specific occasions in the last six weeks I've asked you to take on a special assignment and you've refused. Furthermore, in our last monthly meeting of all the trainees, I asked for volunteers to transfer to another section to learn additional functions of the department and you were the only one who didn't raise his hand. In view of this, how do you expect me to believe that you really want more challenging work?"

In both illustrations, the interviewer focused on a point of contention and then confronted the employee with an apparent discrepancy. This is essential to bring these contentious issues to a head. You must address them directly.

**Use.** The final step in the sequence for conducting the disciplinary interview is to make use of the information you have collected up to this point in the interview to meet the third objective: identifying corrective action. Since this interview may be the final step that you take to correct unacceptable performance, it is essential that you and the employee leave the interview with a clear understanding of the situation and a clear plan. Let's return to the three groups of reasons for unacceptable performance and consider how you can use the information you gain in the interview.

1. *Employee is not capable.* If you are interviewing an employee who appears to lack the knowledge and skill to do the job, you must either alter the employee's potential to do the job or move him or her to another job. In these cases, it is essential that you focus and probe to diagnose in detail what aspects of the job the employee is failing to perform and what he or she is lacking. On the basis of this analysis, your plans for change may involve training, a new configuration of job responsibilities, transfer to

another job, or even termination. Before you end the interview you must make certain that the employee understands that he or she is failing to meet your performance standards and why and what corrective action is appropriate.

2. *Employee resists performing well.* These are particularly tough cases. The employee you are dealing with may be quite capable of performing well but does not. As mentioned earlier, while you focus and probe, you will need to mildly confront this type of employee. It is important, however, not to slip into the role of the punitive parent. Instead, you must use what you have learned about the employee's reasons for failing to perform or violating a policy by shifting the responsibility for change *to the employee.* Ask the employee what steps he or she will take to improve. Ask the employee to give you the reasons why he or she should not be terminated for such actions. A useful tactic[1] is to suspend the employee for a day *with pay* and ask him or her to return with a decision to resign or remain with the company and, if he or she chooses to remain, with a plan for improving his or her performance.

3. *Employee doesn't know the rules.* If you learn during the focus and probe stage of the interview that the employee truly did not know what was expected of him or her, clarify what the employee did know and how the employee learned it. Then before ending the interview, make your performance standards and company policies absolutely clear. In addition, be sure to check the employee's understanding of what you have said.

## DON'TS OF DISCIPLINARY INTERVIEWING

Because the disciplinary interview can be a highly emotional situation that can erupt into a major confrontation, it is essential that you avoid falling into traps that will cause the employee to become defensive and argumentative. Here are some pointers to help you avoid the role of the punitive parent.

1. *Don't criticize the employee personally.* Like personal feedback in the performance appraisal interview, making vague, general statements about the employee in the disciplinary interview will get you nothing but trouble. Don't comment on the employee's attitude, don't tell her she's unmotivated, or don't tell him that he doesn't seem to care. These are highly subjective conclusions that make employees feel labeled and personally attacked. Since they are opinions, they are also open to interpretation and debate.

2. *Don't interrupt or argue.* While collecting information from the employee, avoid interrupting and stating your own views as soon as you hear something you disagree with. Doing so will either result in a shouting match or make the employee say less than you need to hear.

3. *Don't do all the work.* Avoid taking a very active role in the interview. For example, do not make all the assessments of why the employee performs as he or she does, and do not make all the proposals for change.

4. *Don't issue ultimatums.* An ultimatum offers just one option, and it will make the employee feel powerless and trapped. Furthermore, issuing an ultimatum places a lot of responsibility on you. You must consider all the options and select the one that is most appropriate. Then you must order the employee to follow that selected option "or else." Finally, if the employee follows your ultimatum and still fails, the employee may blame you for ordering him or her to take the wrong proposal.

## DO'S OF DISCIPLINARY INTERVIEWING

You must be direct and clear to ensure that the employee understands what you are saying. The following guides will help you to conduct the disciplinary interview in a firm, straightforward, and constructive manner.

1. *Do give specific behavioral feedback.* Instead of stating general conclusions, describe clearly and concisely what you have seen the employee doing. Then ask the employee to explain why. This keeps the focus of the interview on facts, rather than opinions, and puts some responsibility on the employee to investigate the causes of his or her own performance.

2. *Do listen.* Listen carefully when the employee is talking. Make a mental note of information you question, but wait until later to address it.

3. *Do draw out the employee's ideas.* You need to work very hard with open-ended questions and specific probes to get the employee's perceptions of the reasons for his or her performance and what the employee can do to change. Employees must be given a complete and fair hearing, especially in cases where disciplinary actions will follow the interview. Moreover, their explanations and ideas may be valid.

4. *Do offer choices.* Adults must be given the freedom to accept responsibility for their own work lives by generating alternatives and making choices. Give your employees the opportunity of analyzing their own predicaments and proposing their own plans for change. Suspension with pay is a good illustration of this principle. You still retain the option of rejecting a proposal which you consider inappropriate. Furthermore, if you approve an employee's proposal for corrective action which he or she follows without success, you can hold the employee responsible for the failure.

5. *Do be clear and direct.* Finally, throughout the disciplinary interview, you must be clear and straightforward. Some supervisors, when faced with a potentially unpleasant disciplinary interview, talk around the problem and hope the employee will catch on and take corrective action. This only confuses and irritates the employee. When you have something to say in this interview, you must say it clearly and without hesitation.

## REDUCING THE NEED
## FOR DISCIPLINARY INTERVIEWS

Disciplinary interviews represent a last resort to ensuring that employee performance meets supervisor's standards and company policy. While some measure of unacceptable performance is inevitable, its occurrence can certainly be reduced. Several steps can be taken to minimize unacceptable performance and therefore reduce the need for conducting disciplinary interviews. Let's consider some of them.

**Make the rules clear.** Far more often than necessary, employees simply do not know what is expected of them on the job. Job descriptions can be found, but they are often too general and out of date. Performance appraisal forms exist, but new employees do not see one until the boss has filled it out three or six months after they have started work. Company policies are described in detail in a lengthy manual but are not read thoroughly by many new employees.

As a supervisor or manager, you must take a *more active role* in setting out the job responsibilities, performance standards, and company policies and rules that govern your employees' performance. Now I'm not suggesting that you spoon-feed your employees. Certainly, you can and should expect them to take some initiative and seek out this kind of information. But you do need to follow up and test their understanding of your expectations. Don't assume too much. My rule of thumb is, *when in doubt, be explicit.* Spell it out. Your employees will perform better and you'll be a more effective supervisor if you give them too much information rather than too little. Further, you take away the naïve excuses supervisors sometimes hear from employees in the disciplinary interview, such as "I didn't know I was (or wasn't) supposed to do that."

**Give clear and consistent feedback.** As a supervisor or manager, you must direct, control, and *evaluate* the performance of the employees reporting to you. If in your day-to-day contact with employees you give them feedback on their performance, you can reduce the frequency of unacceptable performance and therefore the need for more formal disciplinary interviews. Your employees need specific behavioral feedback when they perform well or poorly. Immediate and clear feedback is especially important when employees have violated an important policy or performed very poorly. Deal with the incident on the spot with a verbal warning and some coaching to help prevent similar incidents. Above all, don't shy away from telling employees when they have done something which is unacceptable.

**Make full use of other interviews.** Finally, the need for a disciplinary interview can sometimes indicate that in other interviews you may have failed to meet your objectives fully. It's your job as a supervisor or manager to know your employees. In addition to your daily or weekly contact with them, some of the interviews covered in this book provide a vehicle for you to learn about your employees. You may be able to detect and deal with potential causes of unacceptable performance in performance appraisal or career planning interviews before that performance becomes so frequent or severe that it requires a disciplinary interview. Counseling interviews can also help you diagnose problems such as employee dissatisfaction or inadequate training before they lead to major incidents of unacceptable performance. Finally, effective selection interviews can prevent your organization from adding a chronically poor performer or a disciplinary problem. In short, proper use of these other interviews will reduce the number of times you have to make use of your last resort, the disciplinary interview.

# 7

# *Exit Interviewing*

An exit interview is a discussion between a representative of an organization and a person whose employment with that organization has been terminated. Its main purpose is to uncover characteristics of the organization that may be contributing to employee turnover and to identify factors in other organizations that are attracting employees.

I believe exit interviews can be effective only with employees who leave the organization voluntarily. Most employees who choose to end their employment do so with some degree of ambivalence. Many leave simply because another employment opportunity is more attractive; others choose to leave because some aspects of their work or organization have become intolerable. In either case, most leave with a reservoir of positive feelings toward their fellow employees and the organization. If approached properly in the interview, they can provide information which can be useful in improving the organization and reducing turnover.

On the contrary, exit interviews with employees who have been asked to leave the organization are unlikely to be successful. First, most employees who have been fired have feelings of anger or resentment and are hardly in the frame of mind to be helpful to the organization. Second and more important, whatever might be learned in an exit interview with a terminated employee should already have been addressed in previous interviews. Performance appraisal interviews should have identified the personal or organizational factors which have interfered with the employee's job performance. Career planning interviews should have identified the degree of fit between the employee's career goals and the organization's career opportunities. Finally, if an employee has performed poorly enough to be in danger of being fired, at least one disciplinary interview should also have been conducted. These three types of interviews should have clearly uncovered any factors responsible for the employee's ineffectiveness.

## SUCCESS AND FAILURE
## OF EXIT INTERVIEWS

There are major obstacles between you and a successful exit interview, even when the interview is conducted with employees who quit voluntarily. Employees are reluctant to reveal their real reasons for leaving, especially if they reflect negatively on their supervisor in particular or the company in general.[1] Except in very unusual circumstances, this obstacle removes the employee's immediate supervisor from the role of exit interviewer. Even though their relationship may be excellent, an employee's reasons for leaving often involve, at least to a minimal degree, the supervisor and the way in which he or she runs the department.

Lack of a clear plan and structure also interferes with the effectiveness of exit interviews.[2] The exit interview has a number of objectives, each of which involves collecting information from the departing employee. Exit interviewers must plan and structure their interviews accordingly. If they do not, employees being interviewed may complain that the interviewer was not listening to them, was trying to influence them to stay, or was making excuses for the company.[3]

Who should conduct the exit interview, and how? The exit interview should be conducted by someone who is perceived as neutral, so that the employee can be open and frank with his or her comments. Therefore, a staff person, such as a member of the personnel department, is a better choice than a supervisor or line manager. Personnel specialists have an added advantage of being able to conduct exit interviews with a number of employees who leave. This enables them to detect trends and identify departmental or organizational issues which may be contributing to employee turnover. Confidentiality is also a must. Finally, the exit interview must be carefully planned and structured, and interviewers must be well trained.

## OBJECTIVES

There are three fundamental objectives in the exit interview. They are

1. Collect information about the employee's new job and organization—pull factors.
2. Learn about the employee's reasons for leaving which are associated with the former job and organization—push factors.
3. Promote good public relations.

This list of objectives makes it clear that the exit interview is not simply a housekeeping session. Many organizations have a final meeting with employees who are leaving to arrange for the termination of benefits, collect company materials from the employee, and secure a forwarding address. The exit interview, however, is much different. It is the final opportunity for the organization to learn from its employees.

A resignation often comes as a surprise to the supervisor and other employees working with the person who decides to leave. This is the result of poor communication. If performance appraisal, counseling, and career planning interviews are conducted regularly and effectively, almost all resignations can be anticipated and many can be avoided. Still, some resignations are unavoidable, and the exit interview provides an opportunity to learn in detail why they occurred.

As an exit interviewer, you are trying to learn in the first objective what has pulled the employee away from your company.

What characteristics of the new job and organization did the employee find particularly attractive? Give special attention to

Nature of the work performed in the new job

Fit between new job and employee's career path

Salary and benefits offered

Unique characteristics of the new organization and its business

In part, a discussion of these matters will suggest deficiencies of the job and organization the employee is leaving. It is preferable, however, that you address these deficiencies directly in the second objective. What about the previous job did the employee find unacceptable? In this part of the exit interview you should focus on

Nature of the work performed

Training, feedback, and supervision received

The employee's own plans for personal and career development

Company policies for employee and career development

Attitude toward salary and benefits

The third objective is to tie up loose ends and terminate the individual's affiliation with the organization on a positive note. Employees appreciate the opportunity to be heard and often have many constructive suggestions to make. Providing them with the opportunity to speak out openly gains the organization not only valuable information but also a measure of goodwill. It's good public relations to give employees a final hearing before they leave the organization.

## PLANNING THE EXIT INTERVIEW

### APPROACH

You should approach the exit interview with a clear plan and a well-defined structure. It is essentially a fact-finding exercise. Therefore, as exit interviewers, you need to set out carefully the facts which you wish to pursue in the interview. This will lead to a semistructured interview with a format consisting of the major topics to be investigated.

## BEFORE THE INTERVIEW

In your planning, it is essential that you do some homework. These interviews must be tailored to the individual employee who is leaving the organization. It is necessary, therefore, that you learn a good deal about the employee before beginning the interview. There are four major steps in this planning process.

**Step 1: Review employment history.**   An obvious first step is to assemble the highlights of the employee's tenure in the organization. When was the employee first hired and in what department? For whom did the employee work? When did significant promotions and transfers occur?

**Step 2: Review performance appraisal files.**   Another important matter is the quality of the employee the organization is losing. Is this person one of the top performers in the department or an average performer? In organizations in which employee performance is regularly and formally evaluated, appraisal forms are generally filed in the personnel department and can be obtained by personnel specialists. You may be able to study appraisal forms to detect patterns and deviations from those patterns. Notice the employee whose performance dropped dramatically since having been transferred into another department eighteen months ago. Notice the dip in performance of the employee who was passed over for promotion the second time.

A particularly fruitful section on the performance appraisal form is plans for employee development. Review these for several appraisal periods and note whether they were acted on or whether they were simply repeated year after year. Look for sources of frustration or futility which may have built up in the employee and prompted the decision to resign.

I want to emphasize a point made earlier in this chapter. Discovering this information after the employee has already decided to resign is useful in planning the exit interview. To be useful in developing and retaining a valuable employee, however, this information must be uncovered and used well before the employee resigns. Active programs of career planning and employee development are certainly important and timely sources of this information which can be used to prevent employee turnover as well as to understand its causes.

**Step 3: Talk with current and past supervisors.**    Another useful source of clues to be pursued in the exit interview is the employee's supervisor. Ask supervisors for their perception of the employee's job performance and tenure with the organization. In particular, ask about any recent expressions the employee made of dissatisfaction or frustration with the job and the organization. In addition, ask supervisors what reasons the employee gave to them for the resignation. This will give you an idea of what to expect in the exit interview and what to be prepared to probe. Finally, in organizations without formal performance appraisal systems, supervisors will be the main source of assessments of the employee's performance.

**Step 4: Develop a list of topics.**    Steps 1–3 will provide you with information that is unique to the individual employee who has resigned. You can use this information to tailor the interview to the employee. There are a number of topics, however, that should be addressed in all exit interviews. These topics relate to the second objective of the exit interview, that is, learning about the employee's reasons for leaving that are associated with the former job and organization—push factors. The topics to be investigated fall into five categories, as follows:

A. *Orientation and Training of Employees.* The first year of employment with a new organization is critical. Poor orientation and training during this period are common causes of turnover. In addition, the first few months in a new job or department are just as critical for employees who have been promoted or transferred. Therefore, you should examine this crucial entry period in the exit interview. Probe the following specific issues:

1. How was the employee oriented into the new department or organization?

   a. Meeting new co-workers.

   b. Understanding of the function of the entire department and organization.

2. How clearly were the job and work assignments defined?

3. How much formal or informal instruction was given to help new employees learn to do the job well?

B. *Work Itself.* A fundamental reason that employees change jobs is that they prefer one type of work over another. The job they are leaving may not provide the challenge, autonomy, or variety they want in work. The following matters fall under this category.

1. How much of the employee's skills and abilities did the job require?

2. How varied was the work?

3. How much was the employee able to plan and direct his or her own work?

C. *Supervision.* Personality conflict between an employee and a supervisor is frequently given as a reason for resignation. Often this is not really a matter of personality but, instead, a matter of supervisory style. Consider the following:

1. How did the supervisor plan and coordinate work assignments among subordinates?

2. How did the supervisor delegate work?

3. How much specific and regular feedback did the supervisor provide in attempts to improve employee performance?

D. *Performance Appraisal and Employee Development.* How fairly employees feel their performance is being appraised and how well their careers are being developed certainly affects their loyalty to an employer. Many employees resign because they feel their contribution is not recognized by their employer and they are not progressing in the organization as they should be. In this category you should address the following items:

1. Has the employee's level of performance been fairly and consistently recognized?
2. Has the employee received sufficient feedback on his or her performance to help the employee develop into a better performer?
3. Has the employee set career goals?
4. Has the employee perceived opportunities for career development within the organization?

E. *Company Benefits and Policies.* Finally, there is the concern about how employees regard standard benefits and policies of the organization. Among these concerns are

1. Salary.
2. Benefits.
3. Working conditions.
4. Hours and overtime.

These five categories are by no means inclusive, but they provide some guidance. Not all may be relevant to a particular organization. It is important, therefore, that exit interviewers prepare a list of topics that pertain to their own organizations, so they can be ready to examine the topics in the interview. The topics may be incorporated into an exit interview checklist, so that a record can be retained of what was discussed in the interview and what issues contributed to the employee's resignation. I strongly recommend that exit interviewers record what they learn so that the results of a series of interviews can be analyzed. I will cover this analysis in more detail later in the chapter.

## FORMAT

The exit interview, like all others discussed in this book, is semistructured. There are three objectives to be met and many specific topics to be addressed, but the approach to the interview must be flexible. There is, however, a basic format which forms the skeleton of the exit interview. Here is the format.

1. *Set the ground rules.* As the interviewer, you must remember that employees are doing you a favor in the exit interview. Therefore, you should begin by thanking them for their

assistance and explaining that the purpose of the interview is for you to understand why they have decided to leave the organization. The transcript at the end of this chapter includes a good illustration of how you can set the ground rules at the outset of the interview.

2. *Discuss the employee's new job—pull factors.* It is best to begin the body of the interview on a positive note. Quitting one job for another can be a very difficult and soul-searching experience, and many employees feel ambivalence or even regret about leaving an employer. Consequently, I recommend that you begin with the new job. Showing genuine interest and enthusiasm in the employee's new career opportunity will create a positive atmosphere in the interview. This should encourage the employee to be open and candid in the next section of the interview.

3. *Examine the employee's reasons for leaving—push factors.* Here you are probing into the characteristics of the job and organization which may have prompted the employee to leave. Be prepared to cover the five topics covered earlier in the chapter. In addition, your discussions with the employee's supervisor, as well as your review of his or her employment history and performance appraisals, will give you an idea of topics which are particularly important and should be probed in detail. It is my view that nothing said in the exit interview should be recorded in the employee's file or should influence a reference the company gives the employee. Making this clear during this stage of the interview will encourage employees to speak candidly.

4. *Give thanks and wishes for success.* Thanking the employee for his or her help and wishing him or her success in the new job is a simple and genuine way to end the interview.

## CONDUCTING THE EXIT INTERVIEW

With a set of objectives and a format now clearly in mind, let's turn to the art of interviewing. In the exit interview you should rely on the familiar sequence of initiate–listen–focus–probe to gather the information you seek. As exit interviewers, you have less information to give in this interview than in any other type of interview in this book. Your function is almost exclusively to gather information.

Indeed, the exit interview is essentially two information collecting interviews, one consisting of stage 2 of the format in the previous section and another consisting of stage 3. You should conduct each in the following way.

**Initiate.** Begin the discussion in stage 2 with open-ended questions to get the employee talking. For example,

> "I understand that you are joining a small advertising agency as a writer. What attracted you to that kind of work?"
>
> or
>
> "You mentioned that you will be joining Company XYZ. In what position?"

Similarly in stage 3, open-ended questions like the following are useful:

> "Usually, Bob, people leave jobs for two reasons. One is because another job opportunity arises that is very attractive, and the move you are making certainly falls into that category. But there is often a second element in the decision to change jobs that concerns less than ideal conditions in the former job. What about your job with us might have contributed to your decision to leave?"

**Listen.** At this point you should listen for points you wish to pursue. In particular in stage 2, you are listening for attractive aspects of the new job or organization which were not available to the employee in your organization. In stage 3, you are listening for topics which fall in the five categories of push factors. Remember also to watch for nonverbal signs such as facial expressions or tone of voice which reveal the employee's positive and negative feelings.

**Focus and probe.** As issues arise in the interview that you wish to probe in more detail, focus on them with the nondirective techniques such as reflecting the idea or the feeling the employee is communicating. Then follow up with a question to probe the topic. This technique is illustrated in the forthcoming section and also in the transcript at the end of the chapter.

## DON'TS OF EXIT INTERVIEWING

Because your function in the exit interview is almost exclusively to gather information, there are a number of traps of human nature which you must avoid. They fall into three major categories, as follows.

1. *Don't defend the employer.* As the interviewer, many of you will feel the natural tendency to defend the organization against accusations the employee appears to be making in presenting the push factors. This tendency to defend the organization is particularly strong among personnel specialists who have broad knowledge of the advantages of the employer and state them frequently in selection interviews. You must resist this temptation in the exit interview by adhering to the following:

   a. Don't present your interpretation of situations the employee considered intolerable.
   b. Don't make excuses for the employer.
   c. Don't ask leading questions to force the employee to say something positive (e.g., "I know you were disappointed when Atkins received the promotion, but don't you think she really deserved it?").

2. *Don't attack the employee's views or choice.* Although you may feel that the employee's reasons for leaving are wildly distorted and that the choice of a new employer is bad, you must resist the temptation to enter into a debate. As valid as your views may be, it is simply not useful to express them in the exit interview; you are too late. Bite your tongue and live by the following rules:

   a. Don't challenge the employee's opinions.
   b. Don't attack the competition.
   c. Don't argue with the employee.

*3. Don't attempt to rescue the employee.* You may also want to try to convince the employee to give the job and organization one last chance. This desire may be particularly great if the employee's reasons for leaving are valid. Perhaps the performance appraisal system is too subjective and the quality of his or her work has gone unrecognized. Perhaps the job was poorly defined when the employee joined the new department, and this caused the employee's performance to suffer. As a personnel specialist you may have been aware of these deficiencies, and you may be quite frustrated that they have led to another resignation. But these matters should have been uncovered and addressed *before the employee resigned.* There is little you can say now to convince the employee to stay. So please adhere to the following:

a. Don't try to talk the employee out of leaving.
b. Don't attempt to provide career counseling.

## DO'S OF EXIT INTERVIEWING

What's left for you to do in the exit interview? Basically, the do's are straightforward and will demand much of you. Let's consider them now.

*1. Do listen 80 percent of the time.* As I have already emphasized, your primary purpose in the exit interview is to collect information.

*2. Do rely heavily on nondirective techniques.* Since you will be listening so much in the interview, it is necessary to encourage the employee to continue talking. Maintaining good eye contact, reflecting ideas and feelings, and summarizing will be useful in keeping the employee talking.

*3. Do listen for sensitive topics and feelings to be probed.* Encouraging employees to reveal their real reasons for leaving an organization is crucial in the exit interview. As an interviewer, you have to listen very carefully for signs of dissatisfaction and then focus on them for further probing. Reflecting these feelings is a useful way to focus on them. Consider the example following:

EMPLOYEE:   "Basically, I liked the work I did here."

INTERVIEWER:   "The tone of your voice suggests that there's a 'but' at the end of that sentence."

EMPLOYEE:   "Well, I just didn't get much support."

INTERVIEWER:   "That can be a pretty lonely feeling. You mentioned earlier that the new job provided an opportunity for you to be recognized in your work. Could you have received more recognition here?"

Notice how the interviewer uses information about the attractiveness of the new job to probe a source of dissatisfaction with the former job.

EMPLOYEE:   "I'll say. She'll never know how much harder I would have worked if she had only commented on what I did well."

This probing uncovered the habit this employee's supervisor had of criticizing but never praising.

4. *Do cover topics on your checklist.* In the first three "do's" you are primarily nondirective in your approach, allowing the employee to raise topics spontaneously. This approach is appropriate in the early stages of phase 2 of the format (discuss the employee's new job—pull factors) and in phase 3 (examine the employee's reasons for leaving—push factors). Later in phase 3, however, you should become more directive. As exit interviewers, you should raise the potential push factors which have not already been raised by the employee.

5. *Do keep the interview constructive.* Another way in which you can be directive in the exit interview is to prevent it from becoming a complaint session. This takes a good degree of sensitivity. You must allow the employee to express anger or frustration initially, but you must strive to avoid repetitive complaining about the source of the anger or frustration. One way of doing so is to ask the employee for suggestions to correct the problem. For example,

EMPLOYEE:   ". . . and one of the biggest causes of low morale among the secretaries is the job evaluation system."

INTERVIEWER: "In what way?"

EMPLOYEE: "It's just not fair. My job was a grade 3 and a secretary in the sales department doing the same job is a grade 4. That was a difference of $75 a month in pay."

INTERVIEWER: "That's quite a difference."

EMPLOYEE: "I'll say it is. I pointed this out to my supervisor and asked that my job be moved to grade 4, but he said it was impossible. Well, I know better. Three years ago in sales the supervisors made a deal with personnel and got all the clerical jobs upgraded. You'd be shocked to learn how many of the secretaries are upset about this. After I resigned, six others came up to me and said they'd quit in a minute if they had another job opportunity. This company just doesn't seem to care about its employees."

INTERVIEWER: "I can see why you would be upset about the job evaluation system. Tell me, Lois, what would you suggest the company do about it?"

EMPLOYEE: "I think you should revise the whole system. It's been around for ten years, and I've heard of all kinds of special deals being made by department managers to get their employees' jobs upgraded. I think you should throw the whole mess out and develop a fair system. At least the employees would get the idea that the company cares about their morale."

The request for a suggestion not only cut short the series of complaints but also produced a useful proposal.

## AFTER THE INTERVIEW

The exit interview meets the very important objective of promoting public relations by ending an individual's employment on a positive and caring note. But the primary purpose is to serve the organization. It is through exit interviews that key people in the organization can learn about the causes of employee turnover which exist within the organization and take steps to deal with these causes. This requires that much be done after the exit interview has been completed.

**Record the employee's reasons for leaving.** As I have already said, exit interviewers should prepare a list of topics which may force employees to leave the organization, and I have listed five categories of topics as a guide. I recommend that these topics be included in a printed exit interview form on which you tally the employee's responses. It may be appropriate for you to design a form that includes topics of particular relevance to your organization. In addition to the outline presented in this chapter, you may wish to review other standardized exit interview guides.[4] Remember to maintain the employee's anonymity by recording the employee's reasons for leaving but not the employee's name.

**Validate employee comments against other information.** Next, you should compare the push factors the employee gave for leaving the organization with the research you did in preparation for the interview. Look for inconsistencies between performance appraisal files, supervisors' comments, and the employee's views. What are the areas of disagreement and agreement? Sometimes employees rationalize their decision to resign by distorting their perception of the conditions of their employment. On the other hand, it may be a supervisor who is reluctant to admit to the facts. Look for patterns among all the sources of information regarding why the employee resigned, and make conclusions based on that information.

**Analyze many exit interviews for general trends.** The next step to be taken after exit interviews is to use the information about push factors as a basis for diagnosing units within the organization or the entire organization. In analyzing a number of individual interviews, look for recurring themes which point to major organizational factors which may be pushing employees toward resignation. Some of these factors may be attributable to a specific department or manager; others may be typical of the organization as a whole. Personnel specialists who conduct exit interviews should prepare an organizational or departmental score card with information on the five factors listed, plus any others which are unique to their organization:

1. Orientation and training of employees
2. Work itself
3. Supervision

4. Performance appraisal and employee development

5. Company benefits and policies

How the organization scores on these factors is a measure of how effectively human resources are being matched to jobs. It is also a measure of how various organizational factors are contributing to or interfering with the effectiveness and satisfaction of people employed in the organization. Of course, exit interviews uncover a sample of employee attitudes which are probably more negative than those of current employees. But they also point to potential trouble spots in the organization which you may need to investigate more thoroughly.

**Take corrective action.** The final step after the exit interview is to use your diagnostic information to have a positive impact on the organization. Begin by identifying the push factors that can be changed and those factors that are unavoidable in your type of organization. Then go to the source of each push factor that can be altered and present the symptoms you have drawn from a number of exit interviews. For example, if employees state that they are leaving your organization for better salaries elsewhere, you would report that information to the salary administration group. If four employees from the same department have complained in exit interviews of poor work planning and little feedback on their performance, you would meet with the appropriate supervisor or department head to discuss these potential push factors.

It is essential, however, that you approach these meetings in a non-threatening, constructive manner. They are very much like a counseling interview initiated by the counselor rather than by the client (see Chapter 4). Describe the potential push factors mentioned in your exit interviews and ask for the view of the staff specialist, supervisor, or department head with whom you are meeting. Confer with that person to try to determine the validity of the information you learned in the exit interviews. Finally, if there is agreement on the push factors, work together to identify potential solutions. Try to consider more than one option that would decrease the effect of the push factors and reduce employee turnover.

## AN OUNCE OF PREVENTION

Exit interviews can identify ways in which the organization is failing to promote employee effectiveness and satisfaction, if they are conducted and analyzed in the ways I have described. But, as valuable as this information is, it is gathered too late to salvage the employee who has resigned. There is much that you managers and personnel specialists can learn from your employees. Much turnover could be prevented if you would skillfully and regularly listen to your employees. A good deal of this listening can be done in the interviews I have dealt with in this book. Certainly performance appraisal, counseling, and career planning interviews are crucial methods to reading the pulse of the organization's employees. It is my hope that, if these interviews are conducted properly, and the information gained in them is used constructively, the organization as well as its employees will benefit, and there will be fewer exit interviews to conduct.

## INTERVIEW TRANSCRIPT

The following is an exit interview of an employee who has just resigned from a medium-sized hospital. Janet worked for the director of public relations who is responsible for informing the hospital staff and surrounding community of the hospital's services and for coordinating fund-raising activities for the hospital. Since Janet and the director constituted the entire Public Relations Department, Janet's job was to assist the director in whatever ways were necessary. Janet's main work has been to do interviewing, writing, and photography for the hospital's two monthly publications. She has also done secretarial work when necessary. After eighteen months with the hospital, Janet has resigned to join a small advertising agency. Since the current director of public relations joined the hospital five years ago, she has had three assistants, none of whom has stayed for more than two years. Sue, the hospital's personnel manager, is interviewing Janet. This transcript is somewhat shorter than an actual exit interview, but it gives the essential elements of an exit interview.

## BEFORE THE INTERVIEW

In reviewing Janet's recent work history, Sue found that Janet received her BA in English and worked for two years as a writer for an industrial newspaper before joining the hospital. She has received no promotions and one standard raise during her tenure with the hospital.

Sue reviewed Janet's first performance appraisal and found that the director of public relations rated Janet very high in the technical areas of her work, such as writing, editing, and photography. There was one low rating in "interpersonal skills." In a recent interview with Sue, the director said that her working relationship with Janet was better but still somewhat strained. She added that Janet's technical work continued to be excellent, although Janet was prone to miss deadlines set by the director. One final point: Because of the work Janet does with hospital staff in preparing the internal hospital publication, she is well known throughout the hospital. It is Sue's perception that Janet works well with other hospital staff and is very well liked. She has heard a lot of concern regarding Janet's resignation. With this information, Sue enters the exit interview with Janet.

SUE:    "I certainly appreciate your taking the time to meet with me today, Janet. As I said on Friday, I try to interview every employee who leaves the hospital. There are a number of reasons why people change jobs, and in discussing these reasons I can often learn ways in which we can make the hospital a more attractive place to work.

I'd like to begin by learning a bit more about your new job. What will you be doing for the advertising agency?"

JANET:    "Well, my job title is writer, and I'll be working with a project group in the agency on various assignments like company brochures, ads, annual reports, etc."

SUE:    "You sound really enthusiastic about it."

JANET:    "I am. It's a small agency so I'll get a chance to work on a lot of different kinds of projects. Also I like the idea of the project team. We'll begin by planning a schedule for the assignment and then we'll work together, building on one another's ideas. This way I'll get a lot of feedback on my work while it's in progress."

Janet has raised two potential reasons for her leaving the hospital: lack of variety in her work and lack of feedback on her work by other professionals. Sue will probe these later in the interview when examining the push factors.

SUE:  "I gather you like the idea of the small agency."

JANET:  "Oh yes, it's a very informal atmosphere. And I feel I can really learn from the people there. As part of the selection process, I had to design a company brochure. The person who interviewed me reviewed three drafts I produced and taught me a lot. He was extremely helpful and supportive."

SUE:  "That's interesting. It sounds like you're feeling very much at home already."

JANET:  "I have met most of the staff and they seem very competent and friendly."

SUE:  "What are your long-range plans with the agency?"

JANET:  "I want to learn about all the aspects of advertising—photography, writing, layout—and then move up to a project group leader. After that, who knows? Maybe I'll go out on my own!"

SUE:  "That would be a big step, and a courageous one."

JANET:  "Well, Sue, I want a chance to do my own work and be held responsible for it. I have a lot to learn in this business. As an English major and photographer by hobby, I'm hardly a seasoned professional. I want to learn as much as I can and see how good I really am."

Here, again, Janet is alluding to her need for training, guidance, and feedback in her work. This may have been lacking at the hospital.

SUE:  "The job with the agency certainly sounds like a good opportunity for you to learn more, Janet. It's an exciting prospect and I certainly wish you luck."

JANET:  "Thank you very much, Sue. I'll certainly miss the hospital, but this is a marvelous opportunity."

SUE:  "We'll certainly miss you as well. You've done fine work here. I would like to spend some time talking about your job and the hospital in general. I will hold your comments in complete confidence, so I would appreciate your being candid. Was there anything about your work situation here that made you inclined to look elsewhere?"

## Sue now turns to push factors which contributed to Janet's resignation.

JANET: "I really think my major reason for resigning was this better opportunity elsewhere."

SUE: "Were you looking for a job?"

JANET: "Well yes, actually, I was."

SUE: "If you were looking around, you probably weren't completely satisfied here at the hospital. Of course, few people are totally satisfied in any job. What did you find lacking in your work here at the hospital? Let's begin with the job itself."

JANET: "Well, basically I liked most of the work. The writing and photography were great, but I'm not a secretary."

SUE: "You weren't happy with the secretarial work you had to do for the director?"

JANET: "No. It interfered with my other work."

SUE: "Would it throw you off schedule on your publications?"

## Here Sue is tracking down the director's comment about Janet missing deadlines.

JANET: "I'll say! I was constantly being interrupted, and the director would change priorities on me. I don't think she really understood how much time it takes to get out a twelve-page newsletter. I'd be on schedule and then she'd hit me with another project. There just wasn't enough of me to go around!"

SUE: "That can certainly be exasperating. How closely did you and she plan and organize your work?"

JANET: "We didn't. She just gave me assignments and tentative deadlines which we never met. Then when I turned in the articles for her review, she would say almost nothing to me about them."

There is a major problem here. Either the director and Janet should have set priorities and adhered to them closely, or Janet needed to set her own schedule and get confirmation from her boss. Regardless of who was at fault, they didn't work well together. Sue probes on a similar vein, remembering what Janet said about needing to learn more about her profession.

SUE:   "How much would you say you learned from the director?"

JANET:   "Really, almost nothing. She would assign me a project and leave me on my own. I learned by doing."

SUE:   "That can be a tough way to learn."

JANET:   "In my case, it was hard. I could have learned a lot more quickly if we had worked more closely together. In addition, she could have gotten a better appreciation of what I was doing and how much time I needed. We really didn't communicate well."

SUE:   "Yes, it sounds as if there was a lack of communication between you two. You've been very helpful in discussing these matters with me. We will miss you here, but I am pleased that you have such a fine opportunity at the advertising agency. I wish you the best in your career."

Sue has learned a good deal from this interview. While she has no definitive answers, she has some hunches. It is doubtful that Janet is weak in her interpersonal skills. There may be some problems in the way the job she left is structured and the way the director of public relations manages. Sue has the following ideas to consider:

1. The director of public relations may need two subordinates—a secretary and an assistant.

2. The director may need to plan and monitor the work of her employees better and to train and give them feedback more effectively.

3. If she doesn't change her management style, the director may need to hire a more experienced assistant who can plan and organize her work with little feedback. Such a person would probably not want to do secretarial work.

# Notes

## Chapter Two

1.  W. D. Scott, "The Scientific Selection of Salesmen," *Advertising and Selling*, 25 (1915), 5, 6, 94–96.

2.  R. Wagner, "The Employment Interview: A Critical Summary," *Personnel Psychology*, 2 (Spring 1949), 17–46;

    E. C. Mayfield, "The Selection Interview: A Re-evaluation of Published Research," *Personnel Psychology*, 17 (Autumn 1964), 239–260;

    L. Ulrich, and D. Trumbo, "The Selection Interview since 1949," *Psychological Bulletin*, 63 (February 1965), 100–116;

    N. Schmitt, "Social and Situational Determinants of Interview Decisions: Implications for the Employment Interview," *Personnel Psychology*, 29 (Spring 1976), 79–101; and

    R. D. Arvey, "Unfair Discrimination in the Employment Interview: Legal and Psychological Aspects," *Psychological Bulletin*, 86 (July 1979), 736–765.

3. R. M. Guion, *Personnel Testing* (New York: McGraw-Hill, 1965).

4. E. C. Mayfield, "The Selection Interview;" and

   E. C. Webster, *Decision Making in the Employment Interview* (Montreal: Eagle, 1964).

5. M. D. Hakel, T. D. Hollman, and M. D. Dunnette, "Accuracy of Interviewers, Certified Public Accountants, and Students in Identifying the Interests of Accountants," *Journal of Applied Psychology*, 54 (April 1970), 115–119.

6. E. C. Webster, *Decision Making in the Employment Interview.*

7. R. E. Carlson, P. W. Thayer, E. C. Mayfield, and D. A. Peterson, "Improvements in the Selection Interview," *Personnel Journal*, 50 (April 1971), 268–275, 317.

8. These summaries are adapted from an internal document of the Packaging Corporation of America, a Tenneco Company, prepared by Richard D. Sibbernsen: 1979; Evanston, Illinois.

9. For additional information, see K. McCulloch, *Selecting Employees Safely Under the Law* (Englewood Cliffs, N.J.: Prentice-Hall, 1981).

10. J. P. Wanous, "Effects of a Realistic Job Preview on Job Acceptance, Job Attitudes and Job Survival," *Journal of Applied Psychology*, 58 (December 1973), 327–332.

11. For detailed instructions on validating selection devices, see "Uniform Guidelines on Employee Selection Procedures," *Federal Register*, Part IV, August 25, 1978.

12. There is a potential problem in this procedure of the interviewer's influencing the performance appraisals to match his or her assessments of the applicants. You might avoid this by having a work associate study the performance appraisals and group them into the three categories. Then you can proceed with the validity analysis.

## CHAPTER 3

1. R. J. Burke, "Why Performance Appraisal Systems Fail," *Personnel Administration*, 34 (May–June 1972), 32–40; and

H. H. Meyer, "The Annual Performance Review Discussion—Making It Constructive," *Personnel Journal,* 56 (October 1977), 508–511.

2.  H. H. Meyer, E. Kay, and J. P. R. French, Jr., "Split Roles in Performance Appraisal," *Harvard Business Review,* 43 (January–February 1965), 123–129.

3.  *Ibid.*

4.  J. G. Goodale, "Behaviorally Based Rating Scales: Toward an Integrated Approach to Performance Appraisal," in *Contemporary Problems in Personnel,* eds. W. C. Hamner and F. L. Schmidt (Chicago: St. Clair Press, 1977), pp. 246–254.

5.  G. L. Lubben, D. E. Thompson, and C. R. Klasson, "Performance Appraisal: The Legal Implications of Title VII," *Personnel,* 57 (May–June 1980), 11–21.

6.  J. G. Goodale and M. W. Mouser, "Developing and Auditing a Merit Pay System," *Personnel Journal,* 60 (May 1981), 391–397.

7.  G. S. Odiorne, *Management by Objectives: A System of Managerial Leadership* (New York: Pitman, 1965).

8.  Meyer, Kay, and French, "Split Roles in Performance Appraisal."

9.  N. R. F. Maier, *Psychology in Industrial Organizations,* 4th ed. (Boston: Houghton Mifflin, 1973).

10.  Reprinted from Maier, *Psychology in Industrial Organizations,* p. 559. Reprinted by permission of the publisher.

11.  Adapted from Maier, *Psychology in Industrial Organizations,* pp. 604–608. Reprinted by permission of the publisher.

## CHAPTER 4

1.  C. R. Rogers, *Counseling and Psychotherapy* (Boston: Houghton Mifflin, 1951); and

W. A. Ruch, "The Why and How of Nondirective Counseling," *Supervisory Management,* 18 (January 1973), 13–19.

## CHAPTER 5

1. D. T. Hall, *Careers in Organizations* (Pacific Palisades, Calif.: Goodyear, 1976), p. 4.

2. D. C. Miller and W. H. Form, *Industrial Sociology* (New York: Harper, 1951);

   D. T. Hall and K. Nougaim, "An Examination of Maslow's Need Hierarchy in an Organizational Setting," *Organizational Behavior and Human Performance*, 3 (February 1968) 12–35;

   D. E. Super and M. J. Bohn, Jr., *Occupational Psychology* (Belmont, Calif.: Wadsworth, 1970); and

   Hall, *Careers in Organizations.*

3. Hall, *Careers in Organizations.*

4. T. Jackson, "Industrial Outplacement at Goodyear. Part 2: The Consultant's Viewpoint," *Personnel Administrator*, 25 (March 1980), 25, 43ff.

5. Hall, *Careers in Organizations*, p. 201.

## CHAPTER 6

1. R. C. Grote, *Positive Discipline* (New York: McGraw-Hill, 1978).

## CHAPTER 7

1. J. R. Hinrichs, "Measurement of Reasons for Resignation of Professionals: Questionnaire versus Company and Consultant Exit Interviews," *Journal of Applied Psychology*, 60 (August 1975), 530–532.

2. M. Hilb, "The Standardized Exit Interview," *Personnel Journal*, 57 (June 1978), 327–329, 336.

3. Hinrichs, "Measurement of Reasons for Resignation of Professionals."

4. Hilb, "The Standardized Exit Interview;" and

   S. B. Wehrenberg, "The Exit Interview: Why Bother?" *Supervisory Management*, 25 (May 1980), 20–25.

# *Index*

Adverse impact, 42
Age Discrimination in Employment
    Act of 1967, 40
Applicants, internal, 21
Application form as interview
    guide, 58

Body language, 56

Campus interview, 21
Career:
  defined, 125
  increased emphasis on, 123
Career development, role of
    manager, 124
Career development plan and career
    stages, 137–140
Career path, 130
Career planning:
  action plans, 146–147

defined, 125
  employee expectations, 123
  employee turnover, 124
  employee's role, 148–149
  influences on, 126
  manager's role, 126
  outplacement, 148
  performance appraisal, 147
  self-interest, 124
  shared responsibility, 126
  work performance guides, 131
Career planning interview:
  career development stages, 128,
    142
  conducting, 144–146
  employee development, 142
  employee expectations, 129
  employment history, 143
  objectives, 127
  performance appraisal, 142
  planning:
    approach, 141

Career planning interview (*cont.*)
  before the interview, 141–142
  format, 143
  roles, 127
Civil Rights Act of 1964, Title VII,
  6, 40–41, 75
Client-centered therapy, 111
Conducting the interview:
  active listening, 11–12
  focus, 12
    conversational tone, 12
  initiate, 11
    open-ended question, 11
  probe, 12
  transitions, 15–16
  use, 12–13
Control in the selection interview,
  27
Counseling interview:
  amateur vs. professional, 106
  approach:
    directive, 111–112
    nondirective, 112
    problem definition, 112
    relationship to status, 111
    tailored to objectives, 111
  asking for help, 107
  conducting:
    feelings, dealing with, 117
    initiating the interview,
      115–116
    nondirective approach, 115
    plan of action, 120
    probing responses, 116–120
  defined, 106
  format, 113–114
  interaction of client and
    counselor, 109–110
  managing, 121–122
  objectives, 108–109, 122
  roles assumed, 106
  sensitivity required, 105
  skill required, 105
  unplanned, 108

Counselors:
  part-time, 106
    limitations, 106, 114–115
  professional, 106

Directive techniques:
  open-ended question, 16
  specific probe, 16–17
Disciplinary interview:
  approach, 157
  causes, 152–153
    reducing, 166–167
  conducting, 158–163
    action planning, 162–163
    do's, 164–165
    don'ts, 163–164
    initiating, 159
    use of confrontation, 161–162
  defined, 151
  documentation, 156
  objectives, 153–154
  performance appraisal, 156
  planning, 155–157
    format, 157
  relationship to other interviews,
    167
  ultimatums, 164
Discrimination:
  charges of, 6–7
    avoiding, 7
  Civil Rights Act of 1964, 7
  Equal Employment Opportunity
    Commission, 7
Disparate treatment, 42

EEOC Guidelines of 1966, 41
Equal Employment Opportunity Act
  of 1972, 42
Equal Employment Opportunity
  Commission, 42

Exit interview:
  conducting:
    do's, 180–182
    don'ts, 179–180
    initiating the interview, 178
  confidentiality, 171, 183
  content:
    guides, standardized, 183
    pull factors, 177
    push factors, 174–176
  defined, 169
  involuntary termination, 169–170
  objectives, 171–172
  planning, 172–177
    format, 176–177
    four-step process, 172–173
  prevention, 185
  relationship with other inter-
      views, 170, 185
  success and failure, 170–171
  using the information, 182–184
  voluntary termination, 169
  who should conduct, 170–171
Eye contact, 56


Feelings of the interviewee, 14–15


Gameplaying, 23, 27


Hall, D. T., 125, 137


Interview:
  conducting, 7–8, 10–13
  content, 7–10
    approach, 9
    developmental sequence, 8
    format, 9–10
    objectives, 8–9
  essential ingredients, 7
Interviewee preparation, 4–5

Interviewer:
  style:
    effect on employee relations, 18
    effect on public relations, 18
    eye contact, 18
    posture, 18
    voice, 18
Interviewing:
  consequences, 5
  effects on:
    employee relations, 5
    public relations, 5
  game playing, 4
  inconsistency in, 5
  need for training, 1
  skill required, 2
  subjectivity in, 5
Interviews:
  importance of, 2–3
  relationship among, 19


Maier, Norman R. F., 82–83, 86
Midcareer crisis:
  reactions to, 129–130


Nondirective techniques:
  conversational tone, 16
  head nod, 14
  pause, 13
  reflecting feelings, 14
  reflecting ideas, 14
  summarizing, 15


Open-ended questions, 16, 53, 91,
      145, 159, 178
Outplacement, 148


Performance appraisal interview:
  approach:
    employee reactions to, 86–88

Performance appraisal
interview (*cont.*)
   flexibility, 95
   problem-solve and tell, 89
   problem-solving, 83, 86
   related to organizational
     climate, 95
   related to supervisory style, 95
   risks, 86
   role of supervisor, 83
   tell and listen, 83
   tell and sell, 83
  conducting the interview:
   feelings, dealing with, 92
   giving feedback, 94
   goal setting, 94
   open-ended questions, 91
  definition of, 66
  and discrimination, 75
  EEO, 75
  feedback, useful, 78–81
  format, 89
  importance, 66
  importance of appraisal method,
    68
  importance of interview
    approach, 69
  management by objectives, 77
  measures of employee perfor-
    mance, 71–73
   behaviorally based rating
     scales, 76
   behavioral checklists, 76
   goals, 77–78
   subjectivity, 73
  objectives, 66–67
   conflict among, 69
   employee development, 67
   salary administration, 67
   tailoring to the employee, 71
  planning, 82
   by employee, 89
   by supervisor, 89
  separating objectives, 70–71
  skill required, 65–66

  work planning and review, 77
Performance review interview, 66

Questioning techniques:
  open-ended question, 16
  specific probe, 16–17

Rapport:
  eye contact, 18
  in selection interview, 27
Recruiting interview, 21
  for job family, 37
Reliability of selection interview,
    24, 62
Retirement and career planning,
    140–141
Rogers, Carl, 111
Rowe vs. General Motors Corpora-
    tion, 75

Salary review interview, 71
Screening interview, 21
Selection interview:
  amateur psychiatry, 28–33
  conducting:
   information gathering, 52–56
   pitfalls, 57
  conversational style, 52
  definition of, 21
  ending, 28
  evaluating applicants, 28, 60–61
   first impressions, 33
   forgetting, 33
   jumping to conclusions, 33
   selective perception, 33
  evaluation standards, 35–36
  for job family, 37
  interview rating sheet, 31
  interviewer attitudes, 33
  interviewer bias, 33
  legal implications:
   basis for evaluation, 47
   data retention, 48

Selection interview (*cont.*)
   information collected, 43
   improper questions, 44–47
   objectives:
      of applicant, 22
      conflict among, 23
      emphasis, 23
      of interviewer, 22
      success in meeting, 23
   performance factors, 31
   personal chemistry, 22, 32
   planning:
      format, 27
      hypothetical situations, 36
      identifying performance
         factors, 34–35
      information for applicant, 51
      review application form, 49–50
   predicting future performance,
      24, 62–63
   reducing subjectivity, 32
   reliability, 34, 61–62
   as a skills inventory, 38
   sources of information, 29
   stereotypes, 33
   tailored to the job, 34

   for trainees, 38
   unreliability, 33
   unstructured, 26
   weaknesses, 24
   when job is unknown, 37
   validity, 24, 62–63

Test, interview as, 7

Uniform Guidelines on Employee
      Selection Procedures, 41, 48,
      75

Validity of selection interview, 24,
      62–63
Vietnam-Era Veterans Readjustment
      Assistance Act of 1974, 41
Vocational Rehabilitation Act of
      1973, 41

Wall Street Journal, 147
Work performance guides, 131–133
Work planning and review, 66